West Virginia UFOs:
Close Encounters In The Mountain State

By
Bob Teets

West Virginia UFOs:
Close Encounters In The Mountain State

By
Bob Teets

ISBN
0929915135

Library of Congress Catalog Card Number: 94-79686

For information address:
Headline Books, Inc.
P. O. Box 52
Terra Alta, WV 26764

A West Virginia Company

PRINTED IN THE UNITED STATES OF AMERICA

Dedication

To the three most important
brown-eyed terrestrials in my life,
Mom, Cathy and Ashley.
And to Mahlon.

Table of Contents

Acknowledgments

With the frantic pace necessary to write and produce this book in a month, it's obvious that a lot of people had to have a common goal in mind, and to then work long, stressful hours without complaint. I would now like to thank these incredible people for an incredible effort.

My Mother, Mrs. Ruth E. Teets, Mrs. Alice "Aunt Al" Spahr, and Eloda Zinn—for taking care of Ashley.

My wife, Cathy— for her patience, tenacity, typesetting and editing skills (and love).

My mother-in-law, Mrs. Emily Meyer, for editing and insight.

Dr. C.B. "Scott" Jones, president of the Human Potential Foundation, for being so kind and thoughtful for the past two years in allowing me to share in the work.

Dr. William J. Baldwin and Rev. Judith Baldwin— for their hours of discussion and support.

Dr. Theodore "Ted" Spickler, MUFON State Director— for help and direction.

Harrison County Deputy Sheriff Gregg B. Knight, who is also MUFON Assistant State Director— for leads and advice (and for great detective skills).

Mrs. Karen Heaster, MUFON field investigator— for her stories.

Mr. Danny Church— for his stories, his courage and for his support.

West Virginia reporters and media personnel, among them, WDTV-TV's John Dahlia, WCHS-TV's Martin Staunton, WVVA-TV's Penny Moss, *Charleston Daily Mail* political columnist Richard Grimes, and a host of other print publishers and reporters— for being the pros they are and for performing outstanding service as Fourth Estate practitioners with open minds.

Mr. C. Richard Farley—for being a colleague and warrior without equal.

Mr. Richard Hopkins—for his printing skills.

Mrs. Susan Williams—for her artistic talent and deadline awareness.

And, of course, to the 150 or so people who had the courage to share their stories with me. Though all the stories didn't make this book (because of deadline pressures), I hold these people in the highest regard.

I particularly wish to thank "Daniel D." of Harrison County and the people of Elk Garden / Nethken Hill. Their stories are important for a variety of reasons, and should never be forgotten. With them and with all of the people mentioned here, I find great strength. Their combined Appalachian character and sense of decency, along with a wisdom and courage gleaned from these teaching mountains, should be an example for all to follow.

Foreword

Aliens, angels, demons or just your typical mind-control or disinformation experts at work?

After reading three or four hundred books, interviewing hundreds of UFO percipients, attending a number of UFO conferences and otherwise intensively researching the subject, I should be able to give you THE ANSWER about UFOs.

I can't. I don't know the answer.

Here's what I do know:

For sure, the phenomenon touches every facet of human existence: science, philosophy, religion, psychology, art, politics and all the rest. It is that centrality which forces the examination of human existence in ways which sometimes confront fixed or consensus reality. Eventually, all of the facets begin to meld into a finite point, but it manages without too much difficulty to elude my efforts to find it. Like a black hole, the phenomenon continually and hungrily pulls everything into itself, even light, never reciprocating.

So that leaves one to grapple about in the darkness, seeking answers to disturbing questions. I've often thought that perhaps it's not about answers at all, but merely about trying to get the questions right.

The importance of the phenomenon certainly suggests that it cannot, for whatever motivation, be free of manipulation, misinterpretation or misperception, or even provocation. There are bound to be rascals—and who knows, maybe even some of them are not in our usual perceptual realm— at work to control or mislead our perceptions. Power and control —both with those who have it and wish to keep it, and with those who don't have it but wish to possess it—are constants in all cultures, terrestrial or otherwise. Sometimes, it takes a war to establish power and control; sometimes, just good marketing. I see both at play in the phenomenon.

Even without a deceitful component, and with absolute deference to **your** own belief system, a serious effort to examine the UFO phenomenon is, in effect, a foray into the **implications** of human existence— clearly a provocative and intriguing, if even an altogether silly, thing to do.

As a former journalist, I find it convenient when working on a story to first try to understand the possibilities and the implications. With the story of UFOs, there is a good tool for doing so.

In 1993, the Human Potential Foundation, Inc., produced *The Matrix of UFO Beliefs*, (see Appendix A). Written primarily by Dick Farley, this document is as good an approach to analyzing the possibilities and implications of the UFO phenomenon as anything else I've seen, so I tend to keep it in mind when I'm researching the subject.

Also, it is imperative that one maintains an open mind when dealing with the subject of UFOs. If you are prone to saying anyone who has seen a UFO is crazy, or is out for publicity, then you're reading the wrong book.

The West Virginians whose stories are highlighted here sure did not exhibit symptoms, as I understand them, of being crazy when I spoke with them. Most of them asked that I not use their real names, so they sure as heck weren't out for publicity. To my knowledge, not a single one of them asked to see a UFO. It just happened to them. And once it happened, they began asking the same question I ask every day: What's it about?

I had thought that my intensive, two-year study of the UFO phenomenon as part of a consulting job with the nonprofit Human Potential Foundation, Inc. might be enhanced if I one day sent out a press release in my home state that requested anyone with a UFO sighting to call me so I could include it in a book. The response was incredible.

In just over 45 days, some 100 West Virginia residents had shared their UFO stories with me, mostly over the phone, and some in person. Many people reported multiple sightings over their lifetime. I added those to the 40 or so cases provided to me by MUFON's (Mutual UFO Network) State Director, Ted Spickler, and Assistant State Director, Gregg Knight, and a few other folks, namely Karen Heaster (Stonewood, WV), and Danny Church (Iaeger, WV). In total, I had perhaps 200 cases in just over a month.

And the phone is still ringing.

Working weekends and occasionally snatching a day or two away from my regular job, I drove my old 1983 Mustang convertible 1,500 miles, mostly on roads that only qualified as such by stretching the definition.

Many of these folks' stories, at least to spit and polish UFO research types, wouldn't pass muster, mainly because the sightings were made by one person. Other stories wouldn't be found acceptable because I did not personally check them out and provide every single detail or subject the witnesses to a battery of psychological tests or at least to a hypnosis session or two.

So be it. To my way of thinking, the best way to research a subject is to interview eyewitnesses. Let them speak for themselves. After all, I'm not purporting to be either a lawyer or a judge at a trial. I'm not attempting to prove anything. This book is not about raw or refined data, but about grass-roots UFO sightings by average folks. It's a brief overview of how the phenomenon touches people—and how they react to the touch.

If an answer to the UFO enigma is to be found, it will in all likelihood come from people such as these, not from a number cruncher sitting in front of a computer, nor from an homogenized research think tank, nor even from some "big name" bestselling author.

And finally, this:

While I don't know THE ANSWER, I do know that the truth is available. I know, too, that the truth will affect each of us in different ways and according to our own needs when it becomes known.

Until that time comes, I feel comfortable with an answer I would give to my four-year-old daughter, Ashley, should she ask about UFOs. I would look into her bright, inquisitive brown eyes and say this:

"Hold a bible in one hand and a sword in the other, then wait to see what happens."

Bob Teets
At home in West Virginia

Chapter One

Something Old, Something New

SOMEWHERE IN WEST VIRGINIA
SUMMER, 1958

The thunderclap jolted the young farm boy from a sound sleep. He yelled and jumped to the foot of his bed where, holding his hands to his ears, he peered through an opened window. He forced his eyes to focus.

Early morning. Clear and brightening sky overhead. A warm breeze curled in through the screen.

He tried to lower his hands, but the cacophonous thunder persisted like the sound of a dozen approaching freight trains. The mounting crescendo seemed surely to be at the heart of a monstrous storm, a twister maybe, ricocheting amid the hills.

The thought of that terrified him as he recalled sitting at this same window a few years earlier with his mother and brother watching a tornado churn through a black night, fingers of lightning clawing the ground and ripping open the peak of the barn roof like a tortuous creature tearing the flesh from the spine of a hapless prey.

He shuddered at the memory— shot another look at the sky.

There were no clouds. No flashes of lightning. Just the thunder, an insidious thing that came from everywhere and nowhere at once to assault his ears. So loud it hurt.

He wanted to run but he couldn't. He felt weak and helpless. He tried to steady himself by sitting on the edge of the bed. To his surprise, the bed began to shake.

He yelled again. Or thought he did. He wasn't sure.

Just then—

Overhead! Above the old maple tree that grew next to the house—
What the—

Time seemed to alternately accelerate then slow, a hyper-awareness which stunned him. Sweat burst out in rivulets that burned like acid cutting lines across his skin. His heart thudded in his chest.

Slowly, a large shape moved ominously into full view overhead, barely clearing the top of the maple tree. Gleaming metal, smooth, with a red/orange afterglow from dual orifices located aft. No vapor trail or smoke.

Suddenly, it streaked straight for the steep hillside not more than 300 yards distant. It was going to crash!

Reflexively, and despite the hurtful, thunderous crescendo booming in his ears, the boy dropped his hands and gripped the side of the bed, waiting for the impact—

He blinked. Then blinked again—

Nearly 95 years before, a dentist named Mahlon Loomis had developed the first wireless transceiver (transmitting and receiving) system.

The signals Loomis is believed to have propagated, received and otherwise controlled through his "top-loaded" vertical aerial (said to have been a large balloon coated with copper paint and grounded with copper wire) were perhaps the first radio signals ever sent from planet earth, antedating Guglielmo Marconi by at least two decades.

With scant financial resources, but with plenty of ingenuity, Loomis used "free electricity" drawn into copper lines from the air to power his signals, just as he had used the same energy to spur remarkable growth and harvest from his "wired" garden and apple orchard.

By the time of his death in 1886, Loomis is reported to have even hooked telephone handsets to his system and established months'-long wireless communication over the distance of some miles. He postulated in his journal the possibility of communicating over vast distances, even with other planets.

In fact, he hinted at the notion of communicating with other entities, as well. For sure, he credited at least part of his inspiration to "Frances," his "spirit guide" who conversed with him via Mahlon's brother, a medium. (As an aside, it is interesting to note that one of Mahlon's contemporaries, Thomas Edison, reportedly worked on, but never perfected, an amplification machine capable of both receiving and sending communications to the spirits.)

Sadly, Loomis had neither the context nor the experience to fully understand his discovery or to properly market it. Several attempts to gain financial backers resulted in frustration, despite his having successfully demonstrated his system to dozens of people, including U.S. congressmen, officials of the U.S. Navy Department and others. Thinking he was crazy, his wife left him, only to later realize her mistake. But it was too late. The inventor died penniless and frustrated.

But not forgotten.

Research to date indicates that Loomis— presumably with the inspiration of "Frances," his spirit helper—did his most important work and experimentation during the 1880's from a location atop a remote hill in West Virginia.

It was the same hill where, in the 1950's, the young farm boy watched in astonishment as a silvery machine with glowing orifices flew over his house and disappeared—*into* the hill.

No explosion. No smoke or fire. It had simply vanished into the earth midway up on the hillside. About where the boy had always gone to play. A magical hill, he had always thought for some reason, though he had never heard of Mahlon Loomis.

A few seconds after the machine had disappeared, the boy, confused and desperate for confirmation of what he had seen, had turned from the window in the hopes that his older brother had also witnessed the event. But the older boy lay asleep in his bed only a few paces away.

Later, the youngster had timidly but somewhat incredulously asked his parents and brother during breakfast if they had heard the "big noise."

All three had looked at him in surprise.

None of them had heard anything.

I never mentioned it to them again.

Whoa, better fasten your seat belt—

— and prepare to launch with me into a possible confrontation with fixed reality. You're about to enter forbidden, unchartered territory alongside a West Virginia farm boy who has a UFO sighting of his own, a lot of questions and about 100 other copilots in roughly the same condition. No one presumes to know the course, and chances are we won't know when we've reached the destination.

Interested?

The only admission charge is an open mind and a sense of humor. It's the ultimate roller-coaster ride— *Starship Earth!*

Come aboard!

My childhood sighting of a UFO disappearing into the hillside of our farm around 1958 (approximate date) was important to me for many reasons, not the least of which was that nearly 37 years later I had some context with which to discuss the subject while meeting some interesting people in my neighborhood of the world, West Virginia.

My first on-site interview took place in what I'll call the birthplace of West Virginia UFO stories, Braxton County, home of the famous 1952 "Flatwoods Green Monster" case. (See Page 11 for interviews and a brief recounting of the case.) But I wasn't bound for Flatwoods just then. I had another destination in mind.

On the hottest day of the year, I abandoned my old, low-slung convertible on a rocky precipice and traveled by foot down a treacherous mountain side where, upon nearly reaching the bottom, I learned from a kindly man that I had better risk the car. "Better to let the car be destroyed than to let yourself be eaten by that big dog that lives on down the road a piece," he opined. I quickly concurred, grunting my way back to the top then returning back down once again, this time in the car.

I then followed his advice to take the first left turn at the bottom of the mountain, because the first right would put me in the Birch River.

He had been correct in all of his assessments.

Biggest damned dog I'd ever seen. It had to bend double to look in the car window.

But it was a sucker for the half of a Snickers Bar I sacrificed to it. While it slobbered and growled at the sticky stuff gumming up its teeth, I quickly jumped out the passenger's door, pushed open a metal gate, hopped back in and drove through the opening.

Ten minutes later, I was on top of the world. Or at least on the top of West Virginia. I could see mountains piling on top of more mountains for miles in most directions. If one were going to spot a UFO in the heavens, this would be the place. Like they say, "Almost Heaven, West Virginia."

David Sykes, 50, had tired of the Connecti-cut rat race as a heavy equipment operator and truck driver, so had decided to find a place as far away in the boondocks as he could.

He was successful.

His 500-acre Braxton County farm, once part of a 1,500 acre plantation before the Civil War, was so far up that he needed to pump in oxygen, and so far out that he needed his own tom cat. Given the vertical nature of the place, if one could roll those 500 acres out flat, it'd be bigger than Texas.

David Sykes outside his home in the summer of 1994. Photo by Bob Teets.

I arrived in early afternoon, just in time to meet David emerging from the house. He had just showered, having earlier returned from several hours in the hay field. He and one other man worked the place. A big job.

He offered a firm handshake, we exchanged some pleasantries, then I switched on the tape recorder and we got down to business.

"OH MY GOD, THERE'S ANOTHER ONE OF THOSE DAMN SHIPS"

David has had four sightings.

"The first sighting was one night about 2 a.m. in 1990," he says. "It's the middle of winter, it was like 10 below zero. No snow on the ground.

"I was sleeping, and all of the sudden the light woke me up. Tremendous light came in through the window. It lit up the house like it's never been— it glowed. I looked out and right on that ridge over there (he points to a mountain ridge about ½ mile away in an easterly direction), it's hovering about treetop tall—it was a ship. It was round and had a little dome on it and from underneath were lights coming out and they were all facing this direction. The lights would hurt your eyes. Everything was lit up. I could look out and see the fields, and see Butler's old barn on an adjacent hill. Everything was silver colored. And that ship just stayed there—it scared the hell out of me."

There was no sound, he adds.

The second sighting occurred on March 15, 1992 around noon.

"This one cow was going to have a calf, and I got her in the barn. Well, she left the barn and she went someplace else, right? So I went out looking for her."

It was an overcast day and the clouds were rolling in over a far ridge.

"I was back in the second field looking over the bank for the cow, and something caught my eye. There was the same ship! It came down out of the clouds, it like broke out of the clouds and sat there for three or four seconds. I said, 'Oh, my God, there's another one of those damn ships!'

"No noise. Then it went down. I figure it was near the Blue Hole (a 30'-40' deep depression in the Birch River, located over the mountain from his property). And it went completely out of sight. The next day I rode my horse over there. No marks on the ground, nothing."

The third sighting happened in February, 1994.

"I got out of bed around midnight and turned on the TV, and of course there was nothing on, you know. I turned on the CB and it didn't come in worth a damn, unusual for late at night. So I shut the CB off and I was just standing in the window there. There was a plane. I thought it was a plane. You know how it will go 'blink, blink, blink?' Blink on and off? I just thought it was a plane coming below the clouds, when all of a sudden that little blinker light went off. All of a sudden, it was another ship! It came right across and went right down to the same damn spot, toward Blue Hole again.

"Later I walked all the way up to Blue Hole where it looked like it landed. Never found a mark on the ground, nothing.

"I told Frankie (his nephew who occasionally visits from Florida), 'They're living underground. I see them go down and they never come back out.'

"You can lay in bed and hear—*grrrrr, grrrrr*—a groaning sound in the ground. Sometimes you can hear them two or three nights in a row. Sometimes not for six months. Then—*grrrrr, grrrrr, grrrrr*. It's like somebody's out here with a big drill, drilling into the ground. I can't locate where it's coming from. When you're in the house, it's coming from under the house. When you're outside, it's coming from under you, no matter where you go."

He says there are no active coal mines close by that could cause the sound. Also, he has noticed several sinkholes around the ridge top where he saw the first UFO.

Members of West Virginia MUFON (Mutual UFO Network) have visited the Sykes farm and have taken pictures of what were reported to be crop circles.

David isn't sure why the ships are visiting his farm, but after his initial fear of seeing the first one, subsequent sightings have elicited curiosity more than any other emotion. His strong Catholic beliefs bolster his resolve to not fear them, he says. "If something does land, I'm not going to try to shoot the damn thing. I'm going to say, 'Hey, how are you doing?'" he quips.

He doesn't attribute any religious significance to the sightings, but says that, "If people ever find out about these things, it's going to put a crimp in religion. It's not going to change my mind, but it will a lot of people's. Everybody needs something to believe in."

David's fourth sighting was shared with Frankie and a friend, Butch, and involved a legend in UFO lore.

Heading into town one night for a few beers and some pool, the trio, with David driving, rounded a curve in the road.

"And Frankie went, 'Holy *!§£! What's that?' And there was a bird in the middle of the road. It had to be— it was so fast. I mean it was dark out, the lights just caught it. We came over the hill and around the corner and there it was. It had to be four feet tall maybe. Butch said it was five feet tall, and Frankie said it was six foot tall. Had long legs, turkey legs, two or three inches around. Maybe a little thinner than my arm. Don't know what kind of feet— I'm driving. And it turned around and looked at us and the eyes went right through you. The eyes glowed, all right?

"And it went, and it turned around and it went up the bank. It didn't fly. The wings put out, but it didn't fly. I'd say the wings were almost as wide as the road, about nine or ten feet, maybe. It was dark, it was a split second. Definitely a bird. Its head was like a parrot. Did you ever see the movies where they had the pterodactyls, you know, those big giant birds in the olden days? That's what it looked like to me.

"Butch never came down for a visit again after that. He's terrified of this."

The sighting bears a resemblance to the now famous "Mothman" sightings reported by more than a hundred people in Point Pleasant, WV, and surrounding areas during the late 1960's. UFO investigator and author John Keel wrote a wonderful book about that case, *The Mothman Prophecies*, which was recently reissued and available at most bookstores or specialty mail-order outlets.

In the book, Keel states that all who saw the "Mothman" agreed that it was "gray, apparently featherless, as large—or larger—than a big man, had a wingspread of about ten feet, took off straight up like a helicopter, and did not flap its wings in flight. Its face was a puzzle. No one could describe it. The two red eyes dominated it."

Keel also mentions other bird sightings in nearby Ohio and Pennsylvania during the same time period (1966-67), including a hunter who saw a 7-foot tall, ostrich-looking bird in a corn-field. The bird did not fly, but instead ran in an odd sidewise motion. An Ohio family reportedly watched an entire flock of "man-sized" birds which were 4-5 feet tall with a wing-span of at least 10 feet.

Another book, *People of the Web*, by Gregory L. Little, re-counts a similar crea-ture spotted as early as 1735; and then, in 1909, another nearly identical birdman, the "Jersey Devil," was

Scanned image of James Rodriquez's painting which was based on eyewitness accounts of the "Mothman." From the book, Redcoats, Redskins, and Red-Eyed Monsters: West Virginia, Its History and People, *by E. Lee North. With permission of the author.*

seen by hundreds of New Jersey and Pennsylvania residents. Little goes on to draw a correlation to what was known as the "Piasa bird" to native American Indians, who painted the likeness of the birdman on a rock cliff, and who used symbols of a similar appearance in various rites.

Dr. Jacques Vallee, whose books on the subject are legends in themselves (see, "Bibliography" for specific titles), and others consider these repetitive sightings as possible archetypal symbols common throughout human history and woven into myths and legends.

ANOTHER MOTHMAN SIGHTING?

On July 7, 1994, "John B." (not his real name), 28, called me to report his sighting.

He was seven years old when, in July, 1973, his family was returning home from a family reunion north of Point Pleasant.

"We were in the TNT area, and this thing—mostly white, no wings, with real thick, shaggy hair—just started floating alongside the car," James says. "We were going 65 miles-per-hour."

Though he couldn't see its face, he said the creature's head was at least three feet wide.

The various Mothman appearances in the 60's and 70's at least had a precedent dating back to the ancient Amerindians, perhaps even before.

But in 1952, and just a few miles up the road from where David Sykes now lives, a whole new precedent was being set for the UFO phenomenon.

Chapter Three

Great Balls of Fire in the Sky

On the evening of September 12, 1952, five-year-old Peggy Harvey Clise was walking toward her grandparents' home in Flatwoods, WV, a small village squeezed between imposing mountains in Braxton County.

"I was carrying a large salad bowl that I was returning to my grandparents, who had previously sent it over to the Clise household full of fresh garden greens," Peggy, now in her 40's, recalls. "As I walked down the sidewalk between our house and their house, I was looking around, and I looked up and saw this huge ball of flame. I started to run, I thought it was going to get me. I was running to tell Granddad to come and see. As I ran down the steps, the bowl flew forward and hit the door of their house and, of course,

The welcome sign at Flatwoods tells a visitor the importance that locals place on the 1952 UFO sighting which occurred in their town. Photo by Bob Teets.

broke all to pieces. They came running out to see what happened—and I was screaming, 'There's a ball of fire in the sky!'"

Meanwhile, beautician Kathleen May had just arrived at her home in Flatwoods from the beauty shop where she worked in nearby Sutton.

"I hadn't been home thirty minutes," she says. "I still had my uniform on.

"Well, it was just getting dusk, and my boys, who had been playing football, came running into the house and said, 'Mother, there's a flying saucer landed up here on the hill behind the house, we're going up.' I said, 'Deed you're not going by yourself.' So there was a flashlight sitting on the coffee table. I grabbed it and took off with them.

"Well, as we got out into the yard, I could see that purplish red-looking flare up there against the hill. I said, 'Now, boys, we'll just go and locate the site of where it landed and then we'll come back and call the law and let them come and investigate.'"

As they neared the top of the hill, according to a newspaper account at the time, "Mrs. May said she saw a huge ball of fire about 100 yards away, pulsing light and making a slight hissing sound."

The group then proceeded on up the hill.

"I kept thinking it's getting awful misty, you know, kind of like a warm mist and looked like it was getting kind of foggy. I remember turning around and looking back toward town to see if the street lights had come on yet. About that time, we turned around and there— we faced that thing— and I turned on that flashlight and it lit up like a Christmas tree— on the inside. It was, they estimated it to be about 10' tall, but it was about two feet off the ground, just kind of bobbing along on the ground and making a hissing noise."

It seemed to be coming in her direction.

When it was within about ten feet of Kathleen, she says, "It squirted oil all over my uniform.

"Well, it scared us to death. Gene Lemon, one of the boys, just fell backwards, then he rolled over and got up and they all took off running. Well, I took off running, too, and passed all of the boys. I swear, I jumped, well, they said it was a four-foot wooden fence, and they said I went right over top of that and didn't touch it."

Kathleen, now in her 70's and living in the area, isn't about to back up from her version of the story, despite controversy about the events.

Some people in the area insist that the sighting was that of a meteorite.

Kathleen swears that Ivan Sanderson, an author and popular researcher of the paranormal during that time, told her that he had obtained radar reports of the object's path, and that it had made a right turn in its flight. She says Sanderson told her, "Meteorites don't make right turns."

Sanderson later wrote:

"In view of the initial reports and our own firsthand investigations and more especially as a result of the plotting of the incidents on a map, we are of the opinion that a flight of intelligently controlled constructions flew over Braxton County, West Virginia, on the evening of the 12th of September, 1952, and further, that two of them landed or crashed, a third crashed, and a fourth blew up in the air."

His references to other "constructions" included reports of crashes or landings from nearby Gassaway and Frametown (where the Minnichs' and David Sykes now live—see their stories elsewhere in the book) and from a report further to the south-west, near Charleston,

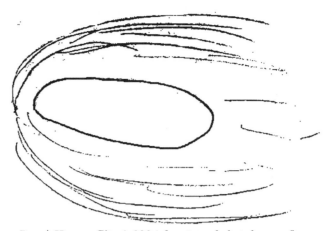

Peggy Harvey Clise's 1994 drawing of what she saw fly over her head while on the way to her grandparents' home in 1952.

where a witness reportedly watched something disintegrate in midair.

Other folks in the area say that Kathleen and the boys walked up over a rise and into an old farm tractor that was idling roughly, had its lights on, and was spitting oil.

Kathleen says that what she saw wasn't a tractor.

For one thing, she states, she was visited by two men who first claimed to be reporters, but who later confessed to being with the government. It's unlikely the government would dispatch representatives for a "tractor sighting."

Secondly, she said a reporter named Stuart (or Stewart) had submitted a request to the National Guard, for it had been Guard units which had initially investigated the scene, for an analysis of oil samples recovered from the scene, and for an explanation of what the government thought the object was which Kathleen had described.

He eventually received a reply.

"Stuart called me and asked if I could have the boys at my house at 7 p.m. one evening. He said, 'I got an envelope here from the government and I can't open it until seven. I want all of you with me.'

"I had them, the boys, there at seven.

"He came out and opened it up, and they had a five-by-seven picture in there of the thing that I described. They said I gave the best description of it, even of those who helped build it. They said it was ships they were building to send to the moon. There was supposed to have been four of them that night, and all four of them came down, but they hadn't been able to locate

An artist's conception of the Green Monster scanned from a March 6, 1966 Sunday Gazette-Mail "State Magazine" supplement which published a retrospective of the famous "Phantom of Flatwoods." Artist credited as 'Lytle.'

this one. They said that the ship that came down was having oil trouble. And there were supposed to be two men in it."

"But what you saw wasn't a man?" I ask.

"Oh, no. They were on the inside of the vessel that was supposed to have landed and skidded on over the other side of the hill. It wasn't a monster, it was a vessel of some kind."

She once described it as being made out of metal, with a head shaped like the ace of spades, antennas sprouting from its sides—unlike the claws depicted in some drawings, like the one at left—and portholes, through which she could see glowing light.

"It was black. But the body part and the head glowed. You've seen drapes? Heavy drapes, how they'll hang on a window? They draped out clear down on the bottom and kind of flared out. It was a metallic green. It must have been metal of some kind."

"After all these years, would you say it was intelligent or like a robot?" I ask.

"We thought it was a robot. I didn't know if the thing would follow us home or what."

"Did you think this thing meant to do you harm?"

"No, well, right at the time I didn't. But the only thing I wanted to do was get away from it. Get back to the house and shut the door."

"Had you not seen it before hitting it with your flashlight beam?"

"We were just curious, so we kept going and we were kind of around a little swag, you know, and we were right up on it, nearly before we knew it."

14

"Then it sprayed you with oil. Where did the oil come from?"

"Came from that machine, that missile, whatever it was."

"Now that's where I'm confused. You're saying the robot is what the government told you was a missile?"

"Yes."

"Then there was something else down over the hill with the skid marks."

"Yeah."

"But you didn't see a flying saucer?"

" No, there was no flying saucer around there."

"You just saw this thing. But it had eyes, and you were within 10' of it and it was 10' high. You say it had no arms?"

" It wasn't on the ground, it was hovering like on top of the ground like it was getting ready to take off or something."

"But it had no arms like it shows in the drawing?"

" No. No claws. The antennae were around the neckline here. The neck, the head just looked like it set down on the body. One on each side that I could see."

"Did you think of this thing as some kind of creature, a monster or something with a brain?"

"That's what we were afraid of, we thought it was something from outer space. We didn't know where it was from. But they guaranteed us it was from our own government."

"What do you think now? What do you think you saw?"

" I have no idea, truthfully I have no idea. We just took it for granted, the government told us that, and that's what they wanted us to know. So ... we just dismissed it from our mind. So far, nobody's had any ill effects from it. So evidently it was one of our government's machines or something. I think if it'd been from outer space, and they'd meant us any harm, we'd been sick or something."

Peggy Harvey Clise remembers this: "It was moving fast... It came across the sky and appeared to go down the hill behind cousin Mary Fisher's farm. I didn't hear a crash, anything. We had a very large hickory tree and it was considerably above that tree, but it burned the leaves on the top of the tree. It probably made noise, something drew my attention to look at it...

"I remember saying to Granddad, 'Come and look!' They swore me to secrecy that I would never tell anybody that I had seen it. My family told me not to tell.

"My Grandfather said it was most likely a meteorite. I don't recall a

Kathleen May (Horner) in 1993 stands on the spot where, in 1952, she and some local boys encountered the so-called Flatwoods "Green Monster." The resulting story was voted the nation's eleventh best news story of that year by various press services, according to Holt Byrne, former editor of the Braxton Central *newspaper.*

smoke trail behind it. People talked about an odd smell that hovered over the town. Such as burning oil or burning aircraft type smell. I don't know. I did not smell that or see anything like that.

"As a child, of course, this was during the Korean War period. This was probably my first thought, somebody was invading us."

It is relevant here to note that a few months earlier, a July, 1952 "UFO flap" in Washington, D.C. included concern of crafts entering restricted air space over the White House, and of several crafts ringing the city.

In view of this, it is legitimate to ponder a number of questions: Given the level of activity which continues in this general vicinity of West Virginia, are there connections to the '52 sightings? Are these UFOs actually government aircraft?

Or, as Peggy Harvey Clise wondered, is somebody invading us?

Chapter Four

Angels, Aliens
Or Uncle Sam

Let's fasten that seat belt a little tighter now, and assume for a minute that UFOs are real.

Who or what could they be? Or at least, who could be controlling the UFOs we see?

Using the *UFO Matrix of Beliefs* (see Appendix A) as a model, the popular UFO literature would suggest the following possibilities. This is not a comprehensive taxonomy, but merely a guideline I use. Some of the entries overlap.

1.) Beings, or intelligence, we normally think of as coming from off the planet— "extraterrestrials"— ranging in appearance and intent from that cute little "ET" portrayed in the movies to your worst nightmare —for instance, the movie "Alien", or perhaps not detectable by human senses or technology, except in limited cases when "they" want to be detected, but who are capable of interacting with us;

2.) Spiritual beings, like angels, with benevolent intent and who can be detected and interacted with in any number of ways by human senses;

3.) Demons, as described in the Bible and other ancient religious texts, capable of doing heinous things, but largely dependent on a measure of cooperation from the host or cooperating human, and who may be able to manifest in forms detectable by us;

4.) Interdimensional beings who may coexist with us here on earth or near to it, but whom we cannot perceive with our available human *conscious* senses or technology, and who may have any intent imaginable, as in #1 above;

    5.) Anomalous "beings," like germs or even "thought forms," that could somehow penetrate the earth from outside or from another dimension or even from right here on earth and "infect" us in various ways, with or without our knowledge, leading to behavioral or biological changes conducive to the survival of the invading entity, or perhaps acting as a "first wave" to soften up resistance for more highly evolved invading entities;

    6.) Various earth governments testing exotic aircraft, and/or convincing—through various mind-control techniques—witnesses that what they saw was a UFO and not aircraft of this earth;

    7.) Humans and nonhuman beings allied to influence human thought and belief patterns, with the aim of social control (hyber-fascism?);

    8.) Creations of, and an act of God.

Okay, you are free to add others if you like. For instance, one could argue to the possibility that information—taken in total— is itself an "alien," capable of changing humankind for better or worse, and certainly not all that detectable as a whole by human beings.

Now that I've stated many of the possibilities I think about from time to time based on various books and thoughts out there, let's see what some witnesses think UFOs are.

FALLEN ANGELS

"I know what they are and what they are up to," says 34-year-old Bobby Matthews of Delbarton, Mingo County. "Altogether, I've seen five or six UFOs. They're fallen angels.

"Also, some of them are God's angels. Sit back and watch—there are things going to happen that people have never seen."

Sometime during the 1980's, Bobby was in his yard when he looked up above the tree line on a hill 2-3,000 yards away. "There were three of them," he says, "at the top egg-shaped, then like a basket beneath. They sat still, totally, then, all the sudden, they picked up and left." Bobby thinks they were "scout vehicles."

ited his progress.

Hovering over a large bank of transformers located at the back of the brightly lighted area and about 300 feet away from Rick's car was "an aluminum-looking thing with landing pods. It had tripod legs, was oval and egg-shaped, and had multicolored lights around it."

The downward cast of the bright lights surrounding the parking area interfered with getting a good look at the ship, but it eventually began drifting slowly away. At one point, it flew over and within six feet of the top of the bridge the trio had just crossed, Rick says, and then it headed off in a westerly direction.

He guesses he may have been able to see the object for a total of no more than a minute, but that the sighting had a great allure for him. "I had a sensation in my body unlike any I've ever felt. It was like at the very base of my spine, it was like a tingling, a rush-type feeling. It was a good feeling, but I couldn't make it go away. It wouldn't go away."

Curiously, Rick's brother, Mike, sitting across from him in the passenger's seat, did not see the ship. Nor did he experience a tingling or other sensation.

"I remember that experience," Mike, 45, tells me during our August 25, 1994 interview. "I remember Rick's enthusiasm about the event. But I did not see it, for some reason. This is no hoax, though. My brother's extremely intelligent. I've thought about it for years. It made such an impact on him. I've always depended on his sense of reality."

Rick says the teenaged boy who was also in the car did see the craft, but I have so far been unable to locate him.

Regardless of what the others saw, Rick's experience seems to have lasted well past the sighting.

Sometime later that night after the sighting, Rick says he felt the need to go to a secluded spot, so, "I went to the top of the highest mountain in the area, North Huntington Heights, and just sat there. I was in shock, I know I was."

Somehow though, his arrival on the mountain top helped to alleviate the shock. The tingling sensation in his spine also dissipated. "I felt peace there," he says. "I felt like I was in heaven. I felt privileged. I was honored. I was blessed by seeing something not many people see."

He thinks he was there about an hour, but he isn't sure.

Time didn't seem to matter.

Chapter Five

The Abduction
of "Daniel D."

Daniel D. (not his real name) is a clean-cut, widely traveled, articulate, free thinking businessman in Harrison County. He is amiable and confident much in advance of his 24 years, with a business savvy he learned from the bottom up while working in a warehouse for a relative who owned a successful business in a neighboring state. When the time came, the relative helped establish Daniel in his own business, choosing Harrison County because of its growth potential.

As a result of living a Spartan existence in a modestly furnished nearby apartment while working 15 hours a day, six days a week, his persistence has begun to pay off with increasing profits, which he plows back into the business to help it grow. Clearly, Daniel is a sure-footed climber on the ladder to success, an up and coming paragon of the American dream.

But he's definitely not had the average All-American-boy background.

Daniel says he has been abducted by aliens at least 1,500 times.

And though he may not be aware of it, he and hundreds of other so-called "abductees" are at the center of one of UFOlogy's greatest debates: Is the abduction experience "real"?

Essentially, the opposing forces in the debate line up like this:

Proponents who say their research would have us believe that UFOs are "real" and, therefore, that the abduction experience is likewise "real," include such notables as Harvard Medical School M.D./psychiatrist, John Mack, and his bestselling friend, artist/author Budd Hopkins (a West Virginian, by the way), and a plethora of lessor-known authors, psychiatrists, scientists, academicians, researchers and organizations (along with an unavoidable and quite vocal legion of cranks), most of whom say the abduction scenario is, in the least, a key piece of evidence regarding the existence of UFOs. There is an inside "mini debate" among this group as to the intent of the abductors—ranging from Mack, who thinks the abduction experience may be designed by other powers to lift our spiritual and ecological awareness through transformational, albeit shocking, preparedness routines designed for higher evolutionary change— to Hopkins, whose books carry a nearly hysterical theme reminiscent of age-old fears surrounding invasion scenarios—"they're raping our women and stealing our babies!" Both men seem, however, to be amiably settling their differences, as each is prone to starting a public speaking engagement with effusive, glowing accolades for the other.

Opponents in the "great debate" include "debunkers" like author/*Aviation Week* senior editor, Philip Klass, and members of CSICOP (the Committee for the Scientific Investigation of Claims of the Paranormal), other scientists, mental health practitioners, assorted groups, and academicians like author/television personality/Cornell University Professor of Astronomy, Carl Sagan, (along with billions and billions of cranks) who contend the abduction scenario, like the UFO phenomenon itself, is anything but what its proponents think it is, and is explainable in terms of currently accepted scientific "truths" or observable, naturally occurring phenomena. When that argument fails, they rely on the time-tested "debunker creed": there is no physical proof of UFOs.

And so the debate rages.

Like combatants engaged in any high-level debate, these warring factions will stop at nothing to bolster their influence while attempting to destroy the other side. Of course, both parties realize nice profits in the process, so one doubts if there is any incentive for the parties to ever join forces and actually address the issues. Politics, religion, philosophy, science and the media are all tools in the hands of these warriors as they battle for the ultimate prize: *your* perceptions.

Personally, and as you'll see later on in Chapter 17, I think the debate is weighted to take our perceptions away from more central issues relating to the phenomenon. As I continue to synthesize my own opinions, I read and listen to opinions of many researchers, like Dr. Jacques Vallee, for instance, or William M. Alnor (a former Philadelphia investigative newspaper reporter-turned-author), or former Human Potential Foundation, Inc. colleague Dick Farley (whose *Matrix of UFO Beliefs* I've already mentioned and can be found in Appendix A), and others. I am beginning to think that some of the various people engaged in the debate— whether they are *consciously* aware of it or not— are vying to become priests in a new religion...or executioners of the old.

Indeed, since public perception (i.e. *your* perception) is so important to each side, you should be asking these would-be priests—regardless if they dress in ornamental robes, lab coats, sports jackets, or space suits—two central questions: *Who* is controlling *them*? And for what purpose? (You may wish to review the partial taxonomy guide on Page 17, and the aforementioned *Matrix of UFO Beliefs* for a list of some possibilities with which to supplement your own.)

THE ABDUCTIONS OF DANIEL D.

Now it's time to tighten up that seat belt a little bit more and to focus in on Daniel D.'s abduction account.

First, though, we need to briefly look at one of the preferred tools some researchers use to probe an abductee's memories.

Hypnosis is believed by some to be the prime tool which can help percipients cut through or access blocked or forgotten memories of UFO experiences. To say that this component is controversial and constitutes another major issue in the "great UFO debate" is to understate the matter.

Advocates say hypnosis is a valid and vital aid for unmasking the mystery of the phenomenon, while opponents counter that it's useless. At the core of this part of the debate lies some contradictory research and differing interpretations as to the nature and reliability of human memory.

I didn't know which, if either, side in the debate was correct, but rather than to sit by and listen while they yelled at each other, I decided in July, 1994 to obtain my certification as a hypnotherapist and to see for myself.

To date, I've only hypnotized two supposed abductees, so I can't be of any help to either side of the debate. In fact, at the rate I'm going, UFOs will have been proven to not exist, or ETs will have landed on the White House lawn by the time I have any substantive observations.

With that in mind, then, here are excerpts from the first hypnosis session I ever had with an abductee, "Daniel." The date was August 31, 1994.

This transcript, beginning with excerpts of an interview and then proceeding with excerpts from the hypnosis session, has been edited for clarity and length.

THE INTERVIEW

Daniel: They let me know when they're coming... I had a good 10 minutes last night. It's the blue light that let's me know when they're going to be here.

Bob: This is fascinating. You're so sanguine about this.

D: They've never hurt me, that means a lot.

B: How do you know? You say you can't remember.

D: The most scars I ever had, I had two circles on one side of my thighs. It was like a rash. That's the only physical thing I can ever remember. If they are hurting me and I can't remember, it doesn't affect my daily life, so you know...

B: Are you the kind of person who needs to have these experiences?

D: No. Absolutely not.

B: If you had a choice would you discontinue them?

D: No. I think it's for a purpose.

B: A high purpose, for the good of mankind?

D: Like to think so, but I have no way of knowing. I think they've helped me in certain ways. I've heard for years that I have to have my wisdom teeth out. One day they were bothering me really bad, and I was in no financial situation to get them fixed, no insurance. That night I was abducted. I can remember, it felt like they were stuffing things on my teeth where my wisdom teeth are. The next day they didn't bother me anymore and haven't bothered me since. This was a couple months ago.

B: Have you ever asked them to fix anything?

D: My wisdom teeth.

B: Did you say it out loud?

D: No, I just thought it. I don't say anything out loud, someone may be listening.

B: Like who?

D: Anybody that doesn't believe or doesn't know.

B: Have you ever found yourself with your clothes on wrong or backwards?

D: I've woken up completely naked and I always sleep in my underwear. That has intrigued me.

B: Tell me again what you saw *through* the ceiling one time?

D: It was a bright light with red and green and blue lights kind of circulating around. It was, it looked like it was taking off. But I saw this through a ceiling. That makes me think it's interdemensional. It was through a physical thing that I saw this craft leaving. But I don't remember anything of the abduction.

B: What's it feel like to be abducted?

D: It's as if they don't take your body, just the etheric part of you. You're weightless and you move with your thoughts. You can be anywhere and do anything nonphysical when you're flying around. It's an incredible feeling.

B: Have you ever had other "out of body" experiences?

D: Yes. I was in Greenville, S.C. and I remember going to see my Grandmother, but she was asleep. That was about all I remember. I had a fascination with Robert Monroe's *Journey Out of The Body*. I read that, did all the practices for months. Few times after that I've been able to do it. Not lately though, I haven't been working at it. I have dreams of flying and stuff. With abductions the vibration's the same. It's like nothing I've ever felt, that's why I don't think they take the body at all. Maybe sometimes...

B: You can go through the ceiling because you're not in physical form?

D: Right.

B: You still have all your sensations when you're "out of body"?

D: Right. No tastes, no sounds....maybe a humming sound with the vibrations.

B: Smells?

D: I've woken up, after being abducted, and there was a sour smell to the room. I don't know how to describe it. Not very often. This was in New York, not West Virginia.

B: What do you think it was?

D: Well, the entity being channeled by my friend, said that their bodies didn't adapt to this atmosphere, so they're sort of decomposing so that they can only stay for a short period of time. When they leave, like the residue from them stays for a while.

B: What do you think their intent is when they abduct you?

D: My friend said that I'm a conduit for 10 or 12 groups of different ET's. I'm sure they're using my body for something.

B: Different species?

D: I guess that's what she's saying.

B: You say this experience usually starts with a cessation of your drinking?

D: Yeah.

B: It's like a signal or something? Is it that strong?

D: The beer just doesn't agree with me. It's like a blue light that's

28

around. One time it was coming through the window. Last time I saw it, it was like a blue fog in the apartment. Real light.

B: When was that?

D: About six weeks ago. When the big guy with the cape and this other one...scared the bejesus out of me.

> **H**ow many abduction experiences have you had?
>
> **M**any. I've never kept track, it's always been so much a part of my life. At least 1,500.

B: Let's back up a little bit. What sort of experiences have you had?

D: Starting early on, about 7, I can remember getting lost in the woods. This was 20' from the house, but I was disorientated all of a sudden and ended up about a mile and a half from where the house was, and had to walk home. No idea how I'd gotten there.

B: Was that your first conscious memory of something strange going on?

D: Seems I've had other experiences. I can remember having other ones earlier on and wasn't conscious of them then, but somehow now, I'm more conscious of them. I can remember them now.

B: How many abduction experiences have you had?

D: Many. I've never kept track, it's always been so much a part of my life. At least 1,500. I can't consciously remember all of them, only a few.

B: How many times a year?

D: I would say at least 20 times over the last eight months since I've been here.

B: Tell me, is there a typical experience or are they all different?

D: They all vary, even though they contain some typical parts. Typical experience is to be wakened up in the middle of the night and there'll be figures over my bed. Or even if I'm in my room. I just have a really strange vibration running through my body, immobile. I can't move my arms or limbs. I can move my eyes and eye lids. I can control my breathing, but that's it.

B: Are you familiar with the terms 'hypnagogic' or 'hypnopompic' episodes? (Reader Note: Hypnagogic refers to that state of drowsiness which precedes sleep. Hypnopompic is the opposite— that state of being partially conscious while waking up. Both terms are used by psychologists and psychiatrists, not to mention UFO debunkers, to suggest that a person may experience unusual sensations or visions while in a state of drowsiness. John Keel writes in *The Mothman Prophecies*: "Bedroom phantoms...are old hat to investigators of psychic phenomena.")

D: No.

B: Okay, tell me what happens next?

D: I remember flashes of being pulled out of the apartment or wherever I am, into a room. Sometimes it's even in my room, they're just hovering over me with this— strange vibration. Nine times out of ten I close my eyes and I'm usually terrified.

B: Have they ever hurt you?

D: No, not in any form.

B: Then why are you terrified?

D: The unfamiliarity, the unknown, it kind of shakes your whole reality of the world as you view it today. There's three types of ET's that I'm familiar with. There's the little blue guys, which I've read about in other books. There's the gray guys, and there's a green lotus-looking guy. Those are the ones that terrify me. The tall, green lotus-looking figures.

> There's a green lotus-looking guy. Those are the ones that terrify me.

B: Like insect looking...

D: They are very much like the pictures in the Budd Hopkins books. Only their faces are longer and their eyes seem a little bigger and they're much taller. I would say 8' tall. I can remember their face, figure, silhouette and their eyes, very hypnotic, very...for me, scary. Their vibration is very different from any of the others. It's so intense, on such a different frequency— that alone terrifies me.

B: What other features do you remember?

D: One blue guy, I was in New York at the time, he was working on my chest. His face was elongated, the other ones are longer, this one was more horizontal, more oval shaped.

B: Do you know what he was doing to your chest?

D: Not really. I checked with a psychic friend who said he was doing like a bypass for the energies or whatever.

B: You have told me that they are using you as a conduit of some kind for energy. Did you ask them this? How do you communicate with these entities?

D: Mostly through dreams. Almost no communication with the lotus guy. He's very mechanical in what he does. The one dream, they told me this was part of an integration for a world being for their benefit, for mutual benefit.

B: They do something with the energy, through you?

D: Yes, I don't understand that. I'm like a barometer to test the ⌐ gies to see what they can bring in here.

B: Have to do with reproduction?

D: I don't think so, not with me.

B: Do you see these experiences and ETs as benevolent, malevolent?

D: They haven't been mean, it's their job to do what they are doing. Especially the lotus guy, they're there to do the job and that's it. The blue ones are sometimes playful and smile at me, I'm comfortable with them. I don't mind...the gray ones the same way, I'm comfortable with them. They're more of a friendly energy.

B: What do they do to calm you?

D: One experience, I was in Washington, PA, and woke up about 3 a.m. There were four or five of the taller green ones, the lotus looking ones. They were working on my body. I was paralyzed and I am not really religious but I started praying. I was terrified. I closed my eyes and then a very blissful state came over me. It was very pleasant, very blissful. And then I woke up and everything was fine.

There have been other times. Here in my bedroom. The green guy came, I knew he was coming 'cause I saw the blue light in the apartment, and I was very excited, thinking, "I'm finally going to get some answers."

So then I went to bed early.

Well, I can probably honestly say I drink too much, but somehow... my urge to drink is suppressed. Either the beer doesn't taste good, or I just don't feel like it. It was one of those nights, I just went to bed and I knew somehow that night they were coming, the blue light lets me know they're coming—sometimes.

I no more than closed my eyes, I felt the tap and the immobilization. I opened my eyes and the guy was standing over me. I'd never seen him in a hood before. He was wearing like a turban and a hood, and it scared the *!£# out of me. I closed my eyes and felt another tap, and my consciousness was gone. I woke up about an hour later.

B: Where do they tap you?

D: On the forehead. Tap with a wand. Haven't seen the wand consciously.

B: Do they wear clothes?

D: It's either translucent skin, they don't seem to be physical, they're more of a light being than anything physical. That was the first time I've seen him wear a turban or a cloak over his head.

B: Did you feel it was connected spiritually?

D: I'm sure the whole experience was connected spiritually. I'm sure there's a purpose. I'm not sure what the purpose is.

B: Have you experienced a kind of rapture, or maybe seen angels...

D: No.

B: You have a drinking problem?

D: I like to have a few beers, I would say I drink probably drink more than most people. I don't know if it's a problem or not. I'm content with it.

B: Do you get drunk?

D: No, I just enjoy having a few beers in the evening. A few more on the weekends.

B: What is the blue one's function?

D: Helpers, very playful. This guy, I call him the 'committee member,' (see drawing, opposite page) was in the corner. I was laying on the floor of my bedroom. I slept on a futon, he was halfway through the floor, the blue, as if I were on a raised table. The green one was also working on my chest. This other one seemed to be the overseer. He worked on a large crystal on top of, like my black trash can, looked like he was working on that. It was some kind of light he was working on.

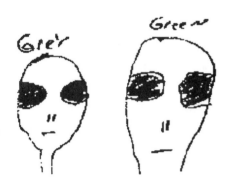

"Daniel's" rendition of the typical Grey and Green aliens he has encountered.

B: Was it connected with you?

D: Don't know. I only felt the vibration on my body. I've only seen the blue ones once, that I can remember.

B: How do they interact with each other?

D: I don't hear them speaking or anything.

B: Do they have movements similar to humans?

D: I don't see them move that much.

B: Do they make contact with each other, touch each other?

D: No.

B: What color are their eyes?

D: Liquid black. This one in the hood I'm not sure of. The green ones, I cannot stare at them. I can look at them and I immediately have to look

"Daniel's" drawing of a blue alien that he has seen only once.

away. Something I can't face, I don't even know why. This guy—the blue one, I stared directly at while he was working on my chest. He was working on me and looking at me, and I'm just staring at him. In fact, I wasn't scared at all with the blue ones.

That's the first time I really remember the blue light. It was coming in my room. I didn't know where it was coming from but it didn't bother me. It was 11:55 p.m. when I laid down, and 12:55 a.m. when I woke up.

This was in Rockport, New York. I was meditating with a friend of mine. For relaxation, trying to integrate everything.

B: How have you managed to integrate these hundred's of experiences?

D: I was fortunate early on to have friends who were experienced with this. The ETs, for one reason or another, waited until I was conscious or aware that it was going on and that it was happening to people before they let me remember what they were doing. I can remember being about 12, waking up and not being able to open my eyes. I think probably they were there, and didn't want me to see them because I wasn't ready to cope with it then. I still think sometimes I'm losing my mind.

I was 19 or 20 when I started having conscious memories. My friend, one of several friends who have had similar experiences, would channel them. We would meditate and then she would channel the ETs.

B: Did she channel the same ones who worked on you or were in your presence?

D: I was witness

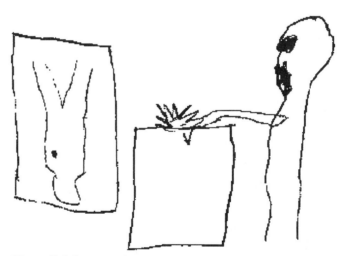

"Daniel's" drawing of one of his encounters with alien beings in his room. In this instance, a large green being which Daniel called a "committee member," stood off to the side and manipulated a crystal sphere while two other beings performed an operation of some sort on Daniel's chest.

to one where she channeled the green one, he called himself the 'committee member.' I asked him why I couldn't remember more. He said, 'It's simply not important.' Those were his exact words, 'It's simply not important.'

B: Does that strike you as odd?

D: They're so much more advanced than we are. I think we're talking interdemensional travel... and the control they have over us. I don't think we have the capacity to fully understand what they're doing.

B: So you're accepting of his brush-off?

D: I didn't like it, but, yeah, I accepted it.

B: Where are they from?

D: I don't know. Never asked. Sure it's from another dimension.

B: Do you feel special?

D: I feel probably it's something I chose to do by being incarnated. That it was some agreement, or some fulfillment to do this.

B: Like, what could that entail?

D: I don't know.

B: When was their most recent visit?

D: They were here last week. They appeared to be working on my liver. Very pleasurable sensation around my liver. I was sleeping on my stomach, which is something I rarely do, if ever. I didn't have the chance to roll over and look at them.

The last time I remember seeing their faces, I was at the store. Very drowsy all of a sudden, and went to lie down on my sofa. Before I fell asleep, this strange vibration came over me and I was paralyzed again. I opened my eyes and the energy was very strong. I could see without my glasses (he is near sighted), which is...I can always clearly see these guys without my glasses, but the surroundings are usually blurry. This time though, I could see everything in my store clearly. This vibration, I felt like I was hooked up to a car battery. It was unpleasant, but it was very intense. Then the... vibrations stopped, and they appeared around me. Then they kind of dissipated or they went through the ceiling.

B: Lifted up?

D: Yes. I could only see their faces. As soon as they disappeared, I was able to move again. There was no waking up, I was already awake throughout the whole experience. I had barely closed my eyes. I was not asleep and hadn't missed any time. The store was open for business. No customers came in. For that time of day it was unusual, for no customers to come in.

B: Do you feel you are closer to divine power...what some people term "ultimate consciousness"?

D: I would like to think I'm closer to ultimate consciousness, but I wouldn't say for sure.

B: Do they have a gender?

D: Seem predominately male.

B: Do they have unique personalities, like humans?

D: I don't know for certain, I believe they do. This blue guy is playful. Grays are six feet tall at least. More of a washed out white. Blue about four feet tall. Cobalt blue. I've never seen their hands.

B: How do they transport you?

D: I just get the sensation of floating. The few times I've actually had my eyes open, you seem to go right through things. Ceilings, walls, and flying down the street.

B: You used to do 'astral projection'?

D: Yeah, the vibration I have when I'm paralyzed is very much the same vibration when I used to be able to do astral projection. It's the same kind of feeling when they take me somewhere. I'm not even sure they take the body, they just take you. My physical sensation is like I've never left the bed.

B: What does the room look like where they take you?

D: I just remember bright lights and seeing them around, that's about as far as I've got. Can't see ceiling, just a big light there.

B: Do you have psychic abilities?

D: I have certain physic abilities. Started noticing them more when I started meditating. I was about 19.

I had an incident in Florida. I was 20. Living in a house with friends in Port St. Lucy. Using astral projection, I left my body, kind of flying out in the neighborhood. And I came face to face with a gray. It scared me right back into my body.

B: Where was he?

D: I don't know. I was going more on an incline, was just focusing ahead and we just seemed to run right into each other. He looked at me and I was terrified and was back in my body in no time at all.

B: Did you take it as a command from him to get back in your body? Why were you terrified?

D: It was the first time I'd seen one.

B: Do you read UFO literature?

D: I've read Budd Hopkins, John Mack. I know about Copely Woods. I had one experience similar to the Copely Woods phenomenon. I was in my store, and had closed early. It was July 3, this year. I became very tired and went down to the bed and laid down, about 3 p.m. I was getting relaxed and a ball of light, about the size of a basketball, came in. Came directly over me and just blinded all my vision, that's all I can remember. I woke up and it was 5:30 p.m.. I felt like I just snapped out of it. The light was there and I snapped out of it. I wasn't tired anymore.

B: When you snapped out of this, how did you feel?

D: Kind of rejuvenated. The time when I was on the couch, I was very much wired, all that energy. I couldn't sit down, I was literally running laps around the store. But this time I was not hyperactive, I was very mellow.

B: Have you ever engaged in occult practices?

D: No. I have no interest. I'm a spiritual person, I believe that the so-called "evil" is within us. It's a part of us, it's our ego. Our separation from God Consciousness.

B: What are your religious beliefs?

D: I was never made to go to church. I can't identify with any of that. I went to a Catholic school for two years, but it had no bearing on me. I believe in the universe, God, the universe. I like to read *The Course in Miracles*. It says there's a thousand paths to God. I recognize Mohammed, Jesus, Buddha. I believe we're all part of God.

B: Do you believe in demons?

D: No. I think we're bad enough as it is.

B: Have you consciously tried to contact these guys?

D: Yes. They don't answer. I can't call them in.

THE HYPNOSIS SESSION

Now that Daniel had offered his conscious memories and thoughts of his varied experiences, it was time to explore the other side, the "unconscious" mind.

After a lengthy induction followed by several so-called "deepening techniques," Daniel appeared to be in a state of hypnosis. I instructed him to imagine that he was viewing a television set that was totally in his control. I asked him to return to the July 3, 1994 incident which took place in his store, and to let it play out before him on the television screen.

Bob: What, if anything, do you see on the screen?

Daniel: Opening my eyes, looking at the lights...feel much like I do now. Notice I couldn't move. I know they're here. And my body begins to vibrate.

B: What's the source of the vibration?

D: I don't know.

B: Tune the TV set to find the source of the vibration.

D: I see the spaceship. Above the store, 20 to 30 yards above the store.

B: Tune the TV to find out what's in the ship.

D: Metallic room. I don't see anybody, I still feel like I'm in the store.

B: What details can you see in the room?

D: Table, light above it. Railing around the side. Looks like there's decks or something below it.

B: Use the TV to look around the ship and see if you can find any beings.

D: One of the gray ones. He's working on a control board or something. Just looks like knobs.

B: Is there a way you could get his attention?

D: Can't move.

B: Now you're back in the store, look around now, what images are presenting themselves on the screen?

D: I'm on the sofa. And the vibrations are intensifying. I'm excited. Very intense.

B: How long do the vibrations continue?

D: Felt like minutes, but it was probably only one.

B: Scan your body now as this vibration goes through, do you detect any particular area of your body where this vibration seems to be concentrated?

D: My abdomen. It's the most intense.

B: Imagine now on this TV that you seen one of the grays, that he has a mouth and he can speak. Ask this little one now what the intent is of this vibration going through your body.

D: They need information. Energy.

B: Ask this gray one where he is from.

D: He can't put it into words. Another dimension. The time and space is just different.

B: Is this dimension coexistent with our own?

D: It will be.

B: Is that part of their purpose now?

D: They're trying to help us to integrate...the species.

B: Their species?

D: And ours.

B: So what is their intent here?

D: They want to help us... clean up the earth.

B: And what use is your body as a conduit for energy in helping to achieve their purpose?

D: They need to know how much energy they can bring in. To this sphere. Sort of a life energy. So they can exist here.

B: How are they using your body for that purpose?

D: They can read the reactions from my body to the energy... through implants.

B: Ask this gray one now if there are any implants in your body.

D: In my chest.

B: When was it placed there?

D: When I was 12.

B: What is the purpose of this implant?

D: To measure the energy.

B: What's it made of?

D: There're no words to describe it... it's more of a thought that manifests as the implant.

B: Can we detect this implant through any of our technology?

D: He's laughing. No.

B: Does this implant bring any physical discomfort to those in whom it's implanted?

D: It's not designed to.

B: Do they first obtain permission from those in whom they implant these things?

D: We have all chosen our roles. Before the incarnation.

B: Look over your memories now and tell me how you made that decision.

D: It was necessary.

B: In what form were you when you made this decision?

D: Spirit.

B: Where were you when you made this decision?

D: It's nonphysical.

B: Were there others around you to whom you spoke when you made that decision?

D: Feel a lot of beings around.

B: Can you describe what they look like?

D: Just other beings of light.

B: Have you all gathered to communicate and figure out a plan?

D: Yes.

B: Was the gray one there at the time the decision was made?

D: Yes.

B: He made the decision to incarnate as a being from another planet?

D: That was his choice.

B: So, this being that you call a gray is, indeed, a being with some physical realities, is that correct?

D: Not in this dimension.

B: Relax... Now back to the TV. Tell me what next you see in the store.

D: It's a green one.

B: What is he doing?

D: He's just looking down... on my body. He's just telling me everything's okay.

B: Can you look into his eyes now?

D: Yes.

B: Tell me what you see in his eyes. (Pause)...what color are they?

D: Black.

B: What is his function here?

D: He's watching over the gray while it finishes retrieving the energy.

B: How does the gray do that?

D: They're just taking it out of my body. He just thinks. He wills the energy out.

B: Where does the energy go?

D: To the ship... he wills it there.

B: Is this a pattern of energy that exists all around us—

D: —yes.

B: —that we have no capacity to feel or measure?

D: Not yet, no.

B: Does this affect you or your physical being?

D: That's the vibrations. No detrimental effect.

B: Somehow your body is used to take this energy—

D: —I just absorb it.

B: How?

D: Must be the implant.

B: Why aren't those aboard the craft able to take the energy without using a human body?

D: To measure our resistance.

B: For what ultimate purpose?

D: The integration.

B: What are they trying to integrate?

D: Themselves.

B: What is the ultimate purpose for this integration?

D: To help us.

B: So they can manifest here, on this planet?

D: Yes.

B: When they manifest, will we all be able to see them, to interact with them?

D: Yes.

B: When is this going to happen?

D: The human consciousness must be able to accept it.

B: What time frame in earth years?

D: Twenty.

B: Given that these beings are so advanced, they should have a fairly good idea of a date and time this will happen. Do they have such a date?

D: No. Has a lot to do with how we treat the planet. Our conscious level, the mass consciousness.

B: Ask them now, how many of them there are working with human beings around the planet?

D: Thousands. Many.

B: Why sometimes do you perceive that they are taking your essence out of your body, taking your soul and your spirit through the ceiling, through the wall, while other times they just visit you in your room. Why the difference?

D: Depends on what they're monitoring.

B: What do they monitor when they just stay in your room?

D: My bodily functions.

B: What is the purpose of the big crystal that the green one uses?

D: To align my aura.

B: What does the blue one do while he is aligning your aura that has to do with your chest?

D: Rerouting energies.

B: Does this require physical contact?

D: Yes.

B: So he has to actually touch you?

D: Touches part of me.

B: How do they manage to immobilize you so that you cannot move?

D: With their thoughts. They're more advanced in mind control.

B: Ask them to show you one of the wands they use to tap your forehead and immobilize you.

D: It's very thin, about one foot long. Ball at the end.

B: What material is it made of?

D: There is no name. It's a thought.

B: This is a thought form?

D: It's a more focused thought.

B: Return to the store (pause)...what happens after the vibration ends?

D: They leave through the ceiling. Just go through the wall.

B: What happens next?

D: I'm able to move again.

B: Go back to the TV. Ask this gray one now, if there are other species interacting with human beings at the same time they are?

D: Many.

B: Do they go by names?

D: No.

B: Ask the gray one if some of the others who come might have intentions that are not so honorable.

D: Some come just to study.

B: Do they come with the intent to harm

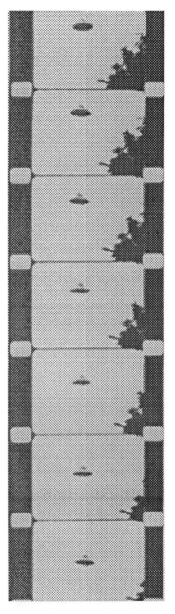

A scanned reproduction of a July 3, 1966 film strip shot by West Virginian John Sheets near Lost Creek, Harrison County. Original appeared in Redcoats, Redskins, and Red-Eyed Monsters, West Virginia: Its History and People *by E. Lee North, with permission. Also appeared in December, 1976 issue of* UFO Report Magazine, © *Gambi Pubs.,Inc.*

humans?

D: No.

B: Have they brought harm to humans even if they didn't mean to?

D: Yes.

B: How did they provide recompense to the individual or to the human race?

D: They haven't.

B: Has their data gathering led to the death of human beings?

D: No.

B: Is this gray one aware whether the Roswell case is actually...

D: The crash in the 40's? Yes.

B: Would that be one of their craft?

D: No.

B: What is it?

D: It's not saying.

B: The all knowing is once again involved here into both of you, all honesty and openness and integrity. Once again, what was this occurrence in 1947 in Roswell, New Mexico?

D: An attempt to raise the consciousness.

B: What went wrong?

D: We covered it up.

B: Did the government actually recover a crashed saucer?

D: Yes.

B: Were there beings inside?

D: Yes.

B: Were they like this gray one?

D: No.

B: Did they die, as we know it?

D: They chose to crash, they left their bodies.

B: What did the government do with the remains of these beings, etc.?

D: They still have them.

B: Where?

D: Say, Texas, but I don't know for sure.

B: What department of the government is responsible for maintaining the secrecy surrounding these artifacts?

D: The entire government.

B: Where are the records kept? In what department?

pened to...he was walking around the living room. He happened to look back and see something. Then he looked again and then he looked at me, and said, 'That's funny, I thought I saw a skeleton standing in the doorway of that first bedroom.'"

"Had you talked to him about the roommates?" I inquire.

"No, he was 10 at the time. But he just dismissed it like it was nothing.

"Then there was the night I was coming home from class when we lived over on another street. For some reason I was just scared to death that I was going to see a UFO or something. Well, Larry had been reading the books about it. When I got into the driveway, my roommate— the one that had seen the kids jumping up and down in the back of his truck— was standing

"Angela's" (not her real name) drawing of a UFO rising above her mobile home in 1990.

on the porch. This thing flies real low above the trailers, and she like, says, 'What was that?'

"I just remember it had red lights on it, I didn't really see it very good and it seemed like it was small or something. We dismissed it. I just remember seeing the red light and it was low.

"A month or so later I had a dream that we were all standing out on the porch. It was me, my roommate's little boy and I think Larry was in it, too. A huge UFO flew over top of the trailer. It had a bunch of little lights on the bottom of it, some were blue. It was huge and I was showing them, 'Look, that's a UFO.' It seemed just like a dream. But, just recently, this lady's little boy said something about, 'Remember the time you showed us the UFO when we were all standing on the porch?'"

"What year was this?" I ask.

"1990. I was talking to the boy's mother on the phone about six months ago. I was telling her about something that happened this past fall. She said the boy has had a really big interest in UFOs. Watches everything on TV about it. She asked him why he was so interested in UFOs. He said, 'One day we were all standing out on the porch and Angela showed us a

UFO.'

"Her little boy would stay with us sometimes. I told her that dream, it's possible he may have been around to hear it, I guess. I don't know."

Other experiences?

"Last summer," Angela says, "in July, I had this really weird dream. I dreamed I was abducted and that they were doing something with my stomach. There was a big red line on my stomach where they had cut me open and closed it back up. I was hysterical and screaming, 'Let me go now!' They were telling me either they were putting a baby in or taking one out."

"Were you able to see your stomach open?"

"Yes, I saw the big red...where they had...I guess that hadn't finished yet, I don't know. There was just a big red line across here, on my lower stomach."

"Any sensations in your body?"

"I was just hysterical. I kept saying, 'Take me home!' And finally they agreed and they said, 'Okay, we'll take you home. Just calm down and we'll take you home.'"

She doesn't recall any more details. But she recalls another episode.

"A few weeks after that, I went down to visit my brother and his wife, in South Carolina. When I was there, the first night, something happened. My sister-in-law has stuff happen all the time, she gets visited regularly by aliens. They abduct her and her sons. All her life. She talked with us about it quite a bit.

"So she and I sat up and talked about UFOs until about 4 a.m. and went to bed. An hour after we went to bed, I woke up because something kept tugging on my ankles. I'd sit up to look what was going on, there'd be nothing there, I'd lay back down again. Something would tug on my ankles again. Right when I was falling asleep. I thought it was the cat. The second or third time it happened, I sat up and looked out in the hallway and there's this blue light coming from my brother and sister-in-law's bedroom. I'm thinking I want to get up and see what's going on. But I never did get up. I just sat there.

Siloutte of one of the alien beings "Angela" saw standing in the hallway at her sister's home.

48

"At one point, I saw one figure standing in the hallway. It wasn't like they really walked out into the hallway. It was like they were just there all of a sudden. At one point, there were like three, standing in the hallway. They were just, they looked like kids. They were all about the size of my oldest nephew. He's 4 ½' tall. It wasn't like they were solid figures or something. It's like they were absorbing some of the light, 'cause they had like a bluish tint to them also."

"What light were they absorbing?" I ask.

"The blue light that was coming from the bedroom. It just seemed like they were absorbing it or reflecting it or something. Made themselves seem like they were blue, too. They had their backs to me, pretty much.

"I got the impression, by the body language between the three of them, that they were confused or uncertain. I sat there and watched them for a little bit and then I like rolled over and went back to sleep."

"You were fully awake though, when you were seeing them?" I ask.

"Yes. I looked over at my sister to see if she was awake and she was out. It seems like my reaction is to shut it out and it will go away."

"Any sensations in your body any of these times?"

"No. I remember thinking how beautiful the blue light was. It was a beautiful shade of blue. Almost like the color of police car lights."

"Do you have children?" I ask.

"No."

"Have you ever been pregnant?"

"Well, that dream I had ties in with more things that happened this past fall. After I came back from my brother's, I was having trouble with a tooth. I had it pulled. The dentist had given me Tylenol with codeine. I was zonked, so I went to bed. I woke up at one point. I had the light on. And something was standing in the doorway. His head was a little bit above the door knob because I couldn't see the doorknob. Was one of the big-eyed aliens. It was brown, or tan. I saw it and just, like, 'Oh, well, that's what that is,' and I went back to sleep. (laughs) I know it sounds weird."

The brown or tan being "Angela" saw one night standing in the doorway of her bedroom after she had ingested Tylenol/codeine prescribed by a dentist.

"Do you regularly drink, take drugs, etc.?"

"Not regularly, occasionally I'll drink. Once

every few months, not very often."

"Get drunk when you drink?"

"Sometimes."

"Were you drinking any of the times you saw these..."

"No, the only time was when I was taking the Tylenol with codeine."
She then continues.

"The next thing that happened, this is really strange. It could have been just something psychological. I had two cousins that were pregnant at the same time. About the end of October. I should have had a period and I didn't. My stomach and my back were just really sore. A few weeks later, I could feel like butterflies in my stomach all over the place. I thought for sure I was pregnant. But when I went to the doctor, they said I wasn't pregnant. We had seen a UFO in the sky right around that time.

"It was, we just saw the bright white light, it would dim down to about nothing, and then get real bright. It was there for a while and just got real small and then it was gone. Larry pointed it out to me. We watched it for a while. Toward the end of November I didn't have the butterflies in my stomach anymore. Just nothing."

"Had you seen any 'visitors' during that time?"

"Not that I can remember. My stomach started getting bigger and everything. I did an EPT (early pregnancy test), and it showed a very light positive response. A local doctor did a urine test, but it was negative. She, the doctor, did the exam and then said, 'Well, your uterus is not really enlarged.' She was a real quack though. She tried to tell me the feelings I was having in my stomach was from my colon." (laughs)

LARRY'S TROUBLING MEMORY

Angela and Larry mention a few other incidents of seeing strange orange and blue lights and of hearing strange "running sounds" in their mobile home. I ask them if they speak about these things often.

"We honestly don't discuss the incidents at all," Larry says.

"Do you think that's unusual?" I inquire.

"I scares me to death, I don't like to think about it," he confesses.

"Why do you read so many UFO books?"

"I don't know, maybe because it's easier to think it's happening to someone else and not yourself. It's like a movie, you're separated from that event."

I then ask him about the experience he had shared with his brother a few years before, and which has haunted him ever since. It had been the memories of that one incident that had led him to call me on July 25, 1994.

He and his brother, four years Larry's junior, lived in a trailer located in a large mobile home park near the West Virginia University Medical Center. It was the winter of 1989.

Around 11:30 p.m. one night, a new snow had covered the ground, so the two decided to go sledding on a small hill nearby. Problem was, neither one of them had a sled.

They decided to use cookie sheets as substitutes.

"We were on Maple Drive," Larry says, "and there was one or two inches of snow on the ground."

Before they had a chance to try out their "sleds," however, they looked toward the Monongalia General Hospital.

"Coming out from behind the hospital," Larry remembered, an urgency in his voice, "was a craft, a UFO. No mistaking it. It wasn't a helicopter or an airplane. I know this sounds crazy, but I kept getting the impression that it was the WVU Coliseum! It looked just like the Coliseum because of the orange color surrounding it. We watched it about a minute, and then it dropped into a valley, and when it came back up, it looked like a helicopter. But it wasn't, because there was no sound."

Larry is agitated at telling the story. He wonders if his imagination has gotten the best of him. He suggests that perhaps the books he's read has influenced his imagination. "My mind is polluted, I don't know what's real," he says.

And yet, he is convinced of what he saw that night.

If this were an isolated case, one would be tempted to dismiss it as delusional, or at least outrageous. But such vacillation is common with many who reported UFO sightings to me. It's as if people would rather believe in practically anything but what they say they saw.

Harvard M.D./psychiatrist John Mack suggests such an incongruous element as this could be a "staging event," in which alien beings employ mind-control techniques to alter a percipient's perceptions of an event. Also a possibility, he says, is the "shape-shifting" ability the beings seem to possess, where they can manifest as animals, or where their crafts can appear, typically, as helicopters.

That Larry first saw a craft that resembled the WVU Coliseum, and which later changed into a helicopter, seems consistent with Mack's findings. Mitigating against such a perception, however, is Larry's own admis-

"Larry's" (not his real name) UFO sighting in Morgantown resembled the West Virginia University Coliseum, pictured above. Just to satisfy our own curiosity, we phoned Silling & Associates of Charleston, the architectural firm which designed the "winter home of the Mountaineers." No one on the design team had ever witnessed a UFO, according to R. C. Blankinship, a member of the firm and one of the design team members. Photo courtesy of the WVU Sports Information Service.

sion of having read many UFO books which could have altered his perception of the entire event.

As Larry, Angela and I continue discussing their experiences, I suggest a hypnosis session, and Larry agrees to be a "guinea pig."

(As in the previous case with Daniel, Larry is hypnotized then instructed to visualize a television set over which he has complete control. I ask him to remember that night.)

B: Do you remember that snowy evening?

L: Yeah. I see it on the TV.

B: Can you see your brother?

L: On top of the hill. He's upset they salted the road because it makes for impossible sledding.

B: Look toward the hospital, tell me what you see.

L: (deep breath) This is not right.

B: What's going on?

L: It's just there, nobody's going to believe it. I guess it looks like two oyster shells, or clam shells. This is stupid. I just want to look at it closer. But, I have to walk behind the nursing home to get a better view.

Ann and Tracy Minnich in front of their florist ship in Gassaway, WV. Photo by Bob Teets

Ann shakes her head. "I know it came down more when he went out in the lawn. It came down enough 'til when that light ray beamed down over him. I saw how the whole area out there lit up. He turned and came back, ran getting 'round the corner in the house."

"We couldn't believe what we were seeing," Tracy says, his voice quickening. "I kept saying there's a logical explanation for this. There was no sound, no noise. No helicopter, no nothing. But it scared me to death."

"It was an eerie...eerie thing," Ann says.

"I never dreamed it was going to do that," Tracy repeats. "We'd been watching it. But when I went out there and then *'Zoom'*— I got back in the house. I don't know, maybe I should have stayed out there and talked to them."

After he returned into the house, Ann suggested they call someone.

But Tracy resisted. "I kept saying, 'This is ridiculous. This is stupid, I'm not calling anybody in the middle of the night.' But then we finally called our neighbors, her sister and her husband, and they came up. In the meantime, this thing was in front of us and in the distance were three orange spheres. They were round and had that same dancing-like movement. And one of them came in close—we have a ridge over here—and it was sort of dancing on top of that ridge. And two of them laid in the back.

And in that same instance, then this thing sunk behind the hill. We watched it go down real slow, it didn't go fast. It was like a setting sun kind of, well, a little bit faster then that."

"It was closer then the ones in the distance," Ann recalls.

"Oh, yeah," Tracy says, "it was a *lot* closer."

Their relatives arrived in time to see the big one going down behind the hill. Then, together, the group watched the smaller orange ones until 5 a.m. or so.

Ann wanted to go outside. "I remember we discussed it, 'It's landing! It's landing!' We begged the guys to take us out. They wouldn't dare."

(It is not very far over the distant ridge to the David Sykes farm. See Page 6 for his story.)

Sometime during the vigil, one of the Minnich's five children awakened and walked into the room... "And here we were, peering out the window," Ann says. "This is the motherly instinct I had. I said, 'Everything's okay,' and I tucked them back in the bed. So I didn't tell them, because I had to protect them."

Tracy remembers some more details. "If an airplane came passing by, the craft would get quiet. The lights would quit flashing. The airplane from a distance would come, and then, when the airplane would get past it, the lights would lighten up and start flashing around again. And sometimes it would get all excited and those lights and everything would really go! Then it would kind of quiet down.

"When it was out there— now we have calves, dogs, horses— there was no barking, no noise, no sounds, calm. Very eerie and quiet.

"I'll tell you what it looked like," he continues. "Sometime not long ago, I just happened to be walking past as the kids were watching a movie, *Attack of the 50-Foot Woman* (starring Darryl Hannah). So I watched some of it. And the craft I saw was just like the one in that movie."

Neither Ann nor Tracy had ever had any interest in UFOs. Tracy says as a kid he was "fascinated with *The Day The Earth Stood Still*. I watched it two or three times." But that's about it.

"What about women's intuition?" I ask Ann. "Anything unusual leading up to that evening?"

"Not until after we started trying to figure out what this was," she answers. "I felt this strange feeling. I felt they definitely watched us, knew when we were moving through the house. I had this funny feeling. I remember going out on the lawn. It was so eerie, because there was no sound, abnormal, animals very silent, very abnormal, and it was a bad feeling. I think there was someone in this, I don't think it was a vacant ship. If you were doing your work and I was standing here staring at you, you would feel me staring at you. That's the way I felt."

Tracy shakes his head. "Yeah, I definitely felt it was watching us. I felt that when I turned off the light, and I definitely felt it when I went outside."

Ann laughs, "And I noticed how the light lit up and went away as he was flying through the lawn to get inside. He came in white as a ghost and I was laughing because I heard all this racket of him out there falling down to get in the house!"

Tracy had not felt any sensations nor suffered any injury from the light, he says, so, "If I had it to do over, I probably wouldn't be so afraid to stand out there and see what it was going to do next. You know, just for the heck of it. I kept saying we will come up with an explanation for this. But we never did."

According to the Minnichs, at least one other person who lived about four miles away from them described the same thing to a newspaper reporter: a bright light with accompanying orange lights dancing on a ridge top. It had been the same night as the Minnich's sighting.

I ask them one final question. "Would you like for this thing to come back?"

"I don't really care," Tracy responds. "We look, we check the sky all the time."

"I don't really want to see any more," Ann says. "I feel like there's been a lot of bad stuff happen to me since that. And maybe it has no connection, but I don't—well, it wasn't so long ago that there was something strange going on in the sky and Tracy was laughing and said, 'Well, maybe we got another UFO. Maybe we should look.' I said, 'I don't want to see anything.' I turned over and put my head under the pillow."

Chapter Eight

It's UFO Season
South In Iaeger

McDowell County is as far south as you can travel in West Virginia. An inch further and you're in Rebel country, Virginia.

Not that the folks in this part of the Mountain State were all that obvious with their sentiments back during the Civil War— or even afterward. It was in this region that "the largest insurrection since the Civil War" occurred in 1920. The so-called "West Virginia Mine War" in 1920-21, according to author Lon Savage in his book, *Thunder in the Mountains*, was a rebellion where "some seven to ten thousand coal miners took up arms against their state and local governments and marched, in defiance of a Presidential ultimatum, against an army of some two thousand state constabulary, deputy sheriffs and volunteers. The two armies collided; machine guns chattered; thousands of shots were fired; planes dropped bombs, however ineffectively; and for a week the miners controlled some five hundred square miles of southern West Virginia."

It took Federal troops to quell the uprising.

Well, it may be time to call in the feds once again—this time, to figure out what's been going on around Iaeger (pronounced Yea-ger). That is, unless of course, *it is the feds* who are flying around in some pretty strange contraptions.

School bus driver Danny Church and his extended family have had quite a show over the past three years or so, and Danny hasn't missed any of it. There have been so many sightings in the area that this guy started a UFO diary and coined a new season. It seems that fall and winter in Ieager are combined into "UFO Season."

Before we get to his story, let's delve into that scrapbook of his for a sampling. (Note: Names have been removed in consideration of privacy.)

December 18, 1992—7:10 p.m.

A group of people were at the Iaeger Dairy Queen when a large craft came over going southwest. It was diamond-shaped on the front and squared off on the back.

February 19, 1993—6:20 a.m.

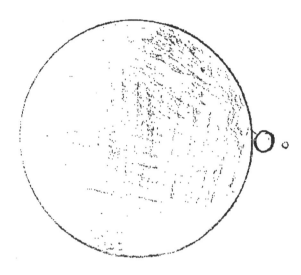

A flying object was observed in the Litwar area by (name). He was going toward Panther on his morning bus run. The object was moving slowly. As he turned the Silo Curve, he said it was traveling toward Longpole. It was a large, round shape. In what appeared to be the front was a large round white light. In front of the big light a small light appeared to be directing the whole craft. Both lights were white in color. The UFO was about the size of a football field. (Name) stated that it was even larger than the coal mining tipple that was below it.

Weather: cold and clear
Temp: about 30 degrees

February 19, 1993

Approximately 10:30 a.m. (Name) was going on an ambulance call on Panther Creek, a place called Georges Forks. As they passed the

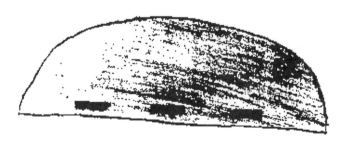

park just on the left going up, (name) noticed just above the picnic shed, that an object was hovering above the shed. It was shaped like a saucer and had red, blue and green lights flashing around the base of it. (Name) did state it was very foggy, so the lights looked fluorescent and hazy. When he turned the curve, it was gone.

Weather: foggy, clear and cool.

March 17, 1993—2:30 a.m.
UFOs were observed and videoed in the Garland area.

March 31, 1993—about 12 noon.
I went to a residence of (name), who proceeded to tell me how he came to see the objects.

He started by telling me his back was hurting. He was sitting in his reclining chair when he noticed a bright flash outside the window toward the Garland Curve. He noticed several huge lights lighting up the mountain top. He called out to his wife, (Name), who picked up the camcorder.

This is what I saw on the video tape. First I saw the street light near the road. But in the sky above was what looked like a mass of metal, brass or copper-colored. It would remind one of a giant piece of aluminum foil wadded up and then straightened back out. As it moved up, it turned into a bright light with two smaller lights on each side of it. Then a long bar shaped-light appeared right above the middle. And then the lights separated from each other. But the middle largest still had the flat bar over it.

Then the largest light started changing shapes, first like a top then like a football; then it looked like there was a bluish smoke or fog coming

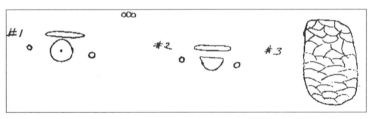

from it. Then the object started moving very erratically, and the smaller lights went off at different angles while the middle stayed stationary.

(Name) stated that while standing there on his porch, he noticed static electricity in his hair. His hair was standing straight out on the right side of his head. This incident lasted 14 minutes.

Weather: rain and fog
Temp: 49 degrees

April 23, 1994
There was an unidentified flying object observed in the Ikes Fork area on a Saturday evening at about 4 p.m. This sighting was unlike the others because this one was seen in the daylight hours. Shaped like a cigar, it didn't make a sound, or didn't have contrail coming from it. The color was silver and had no wings.

Weather: sunny, clear
Temp: 60 degrees

AN INTERVIEW WITH THE CHURCH MEN

I met with Danny Church and his uncle, Bruce, in Bluefield, about 60 miles from Iaeger for this interview on August 16.

Bruce is 41-years-old and lives with his family on Johnnycake Mountain, a few miles out of Iaeger.

Here are edited excerpts from our interview:

Bob: Tell me about your first sighting.

Bruce: First time—we had just moved to Garland, WV. on Rt. 80. Between Ieager and Bradshaw.

I was in church and my youngest son came in and said, "I saw something in the sky." He said he saw something real big, and two or three 'somethin's small' with it. I thought he was just tellin' me one, 'cause he was a young son, you know.

When church was over, I got in the car, and we had to go around a dirt road to get to the house. We were listening to the tape player and he said, "There they are!" I looked up in the sky and there was a real small one. It was high, it's impossible to say how big they were, actually.

BT: How big around were they at arm's length? Compared to your fist?

BC: The small one was just about the size of my fist. I saw it first. It was coming— it was low. It went below the tree tops. It had all kinds of lights on it. There was a little hollow it went up. I had to go through a creek hollow, it was misty, you know, fog laying around on the top of the mountain. I watched it go right up this hollow 'til it went into the fog and all I could see were the lights shining. And that was the first one.

The same night, we went on around the hill and looked up and there's this huge one. I mean it was huge. I'd say it was above the mountains, but when it got...I got to watch it for a good 10 minutes. It was coming directly at me and it was going real slow. And there were lights all over it.

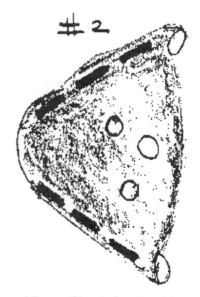

A Danny Church drawing of the craft his Uncle Bruce says he saw on November 26, 1992.

BT: What was the date?

BC: November 26, 1992, 7:30 in the evening

BT: Around Thanksgiving then.

BC: Yes, in the fall. This large one, it came up the Dry Fork River sort of. It didn't go from mountain top to mountain top, so I had a chance to look at it real close. I would have given anything for a set of binoculars. I would've had a real good view of it, it was low.

It was real dark that night but it had so many lights on it that you couldn't see it *per se*. But you could see all these lights shining. It gave you the impression that those lights were recessed back inside it. It looked sort of like somebody had taken a wad of aluminum foil and straightened it out. And when it got directly overhead, it was so large you could just see a little bit of sky on each side of it.

It was above the mountains, it was a huge thing.

BT: The size of a football field?

BC: It wouldn't land in a football field, it was too big for that. That's the way it looked to me. No way of telling how high. I turned the car off and got out. No noise of any kind. No movement. It was around 10 p.m. They first saw it at 7:30 p.m. Wife didn't believe me, but later on she got to see the same one.

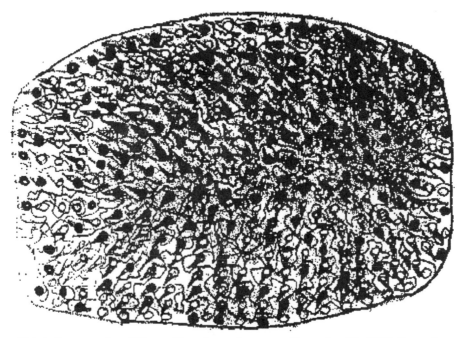

This is the second craft Bruce Church says he saw on November 26, 1992. Its surface resembled crumpled aluminum foil with hundreds of recessed lights shining brightly. The craft, he estimates, was larger than a football field. Drawing by Danny Church.

Another time, I was watching TV and they (family members) came in and said that thing was out there flying around. They used to fly right over the top of my house. It got so regular I wouldn't even get up off the couch and go look at it.

I only saw that large one twice, but once through binoculars.

I was lying on the couch and my wife was getting ready to go to her brother's. She came running in and said, 'Those things are back.' I got the binoculars and there were nine of those small ones at one time. Then the big one came over again, but it was much higher and moving a little faster. But it was the same one.

BT: Any exotic maneuvers?

BC: Those didn't. They would sit down and shine lights around in the trees up on the side of the mountain sometimes.

But I saw one come by so fast I couldn't even see it go. I don't even know if it was one of those types or not. All I saw was a big light go by through the sky.

Some would stop, and go and take off in different tangents. They had two lights on the front, great huge lights. They didn't shine straight out, shined sort of at each other where they come to a focal point.

BT: Did any of these try to communicate with you in any way? Did you experience any unusual thoughts or sensations?

BC: No, I didn't think it tried to communicate in any way. Some other people thought so because the crafts were right over my house all the time.

I have a son who had a stranger encounter than that. David Church, my son. Since the last encounter, he will not go out after dark anymore by himself. He was about 15 when he saw this. He had no fear of the dark before that, but whatever it was that scared him, either consciously or subconsciously, he would not travel by himself any more.

(Note: David's interview appears later in this chapter.)

BT: Does he now?

BC: No.

BT: And this is two years after the fact?

BC: That first time, he didn't get home until three in the morning. I don't know what time he saw it. But after that, he has some indentations on the back of his heels, both of his heels. It's not a scar, it's not a birthmark because they were never there before. They're indentations and they won't go away. He still has them. What it means I have no idea.

BT: Any other changes since that time, personality changes?

BC: I haven't noticed any behavioral changes except for his fear. He's a great big man for his age. He was never scared of anything. But he's not that way anymore.

BT: How often do the crafts appear?

BC: That happens up there every year. They didn't follow me to where I live now, so it's not me. Lots of people up there see them. About 60 miles from here. Halfway between Iaeger and Bradshaw.

BT: Are there a lot of abandoned mines in that area?

BC: No. It's hilly, steep hills and hollows. But right in that area there are no mines whatsoever. They stripped on top of the mountains. Usually after you'd see all these things, they would all of a sudden go, all at once. They'd go round the top of the mountain. They traveled in formations like they were looking for something. They were in no hurry. I would watch them for hours, they'd fly around up there. And after they would leave, a bunch of jets would come in, six or eight jets usually.

BT: You figure these things had beings in them?

BC: In my opinion, that's the only way they could do the things they did. It wasn't a natural phenomenon. They did things like stopping dead and going back where they came from and going off in tangents and joining each other and flying in formation... I saw them make 90 degree turns and go up and never stop. I don't know what they are, where they come from. Whether the government got's something they don't want anybody to know about and they're testing it around here, but I've never seen or heard of anything like it.

BT: What would the people or beings on board look like, do you think?

BC: I don't know. One of my sons was watching through the binoculars one time over on the other side of the mountain. It was flying with a light looking in the trees. He said it had windows and he looked through it and there were people. But I didn't see it. He said they were tall, silver light hair, muscular. I got to the point I wouldn't even go watch, it was so common, every Wednesday night.

(Note: John Keel writes in *The Mothman Prophecies* that of 700 UFO reports he collected in 1966, the greatest number—20 percent—occurred on Wednesdays. "I called this 'the Wednesday phenomenon,'" he states. He claims that a scientist later confirmed his observations.)

It lasted up through March. Summer time came, they'd slowly quit. They've come since '92. Some people have seen them before that.

What struck me the most was their regularity. You could depend on them on Wednesdays.

One night when this was going on, the whole mountain there in the back was lit up, like they were back in there. I couldn't see what was going on because of the ridge.

I've got three boys, Michael (15), Jason (16), and David (17), all teenagers. The wife and boys have all seen them.

I turn to Danny, who has been caring for his daughter while I interviewed Bruce. He is eager to speak.

Danny, 30, lives at Lick Branch in Iaeger.

"I was skeptical," he says, "but interested. Bruce and his family would call me and I would take off flying over there. I lived about 15 minutes away, about eight miles or so. I would watch and not see a thing for months."

But then it happened.

"My wife and I and our baby were driving around this little small road towards home, after a few hours of unsuccessfully watching for UFOs on a nearby mountain. We looked up, saw this bright light. Just a bright light at first. So we go on around this curve and start up the little hollow where we live, we look up and there's this thing that looked like a large Christmas tree. But it's flying backwards, it's real slow, very slow. It slacked up, maybe 200' or 300' from going over the mountain where I first saw it. I jump out, I got my video camera, and I start recording. My wife yells that I didn't set the emergency brake, and my truck starts rolling backwards with my wife and baby in it! So, I jump back in and set the brake real quick. I get out and the tail-end of it's going over the mountain.

Bottom of craft

Path of Travel

A Danny Church drawing of the craft he and wife Betty spotted on Dec. 1, 1992.

He recalls another sighting.

"I was home. My dad and my brother were working on a car, it was in the dead of winter, same year. Very cold, my wife was going by the glass doors in the trailer and she saw it. This object, it was round—but up in it, she said, she could see WAY up in it. It was like a funnel, where she could see the lights, they looked like they went forever. No noise at all. She yelled at Dad and them to get their attention, but they never saw it.

"Did you have any unusual thoughts, as if it may have tried to communicate with you?"

"No. I did not think of intelligent life at that time, but after I thought about it, yes, it was something different from what we have, or what we are."

I ask Bruce and Danny if the jets always came after a sighting.

"Not always," Bruce says, "just usually. Couldn't tell if they were fighter jets, too dark to tell. There would be six or eight of them. Those UFOs would be gone before they got there. The jets were high and moving fast. I got the impression they were just up there flying around looking for something. They'd circle around and come back for about 15 minutes and then leave. I'm sure they were jets."

Neither of the men recall experiencing any lost time during their various sightings, but Danny mentions a curious event which took place with his brother.

"He was in his trailer reading the Bible in a back room. He said it was 11 p.m., and he laid his bifocals down on his Bible. He went to the bathroom and when he came back, he said his Bible wasn't where he put it and it was three hours later. He doesn't know what happened."

"Was he enraptured by what he was reading?" I ask.

Bruce answers, "He said he was of a normal frame of mind. He believes—he doesn't believe in UFOs— the Lord took him and did something with him in those three hours. It's a total blank. His glasses were moved too, that's strange. First and last experience. He doesn't have any physical condition that would affect him like that."

Bruce then remembers an earlier experience in his own life.

"The very first thing I ever saw in my life, I was about 10-years-old. We'd gone to Wilmore Hollow. We were camping out, listening to the radio, when a silver dot flies over so high up I didn't know what it was. It came across blinking real fast and stopped in a beat. I remember that.

"What do you think this was?"

"I believe it's from another world. I honestly believe that."

I ask them if they feared what they had witnessed.

"No, I've never been afraid," Danny replies.

"No," Bruce concurs. "I wouldn't be afraid if one were to set down. I'd try to communicate with it. I don't believe they mean us any harm."

"Did your religious views change because of what you saw?"

"I don't know, I can't say," Danny says.

"I was already saved and going to church when I saw it," Bruce states. "It didn't come as any surprise to me because the Bible doesn't say one way or the other about it. I believe God made all those stars up there for a purpose, not just for us to look at. There's no explanation for it. Anything is possible. I try to keep an open mind. There is definitely something out there. What it is, I have no idea. They are not a part of our world as we know it."

OFF TO IAEGER

I was so struck by these two mens' stories and the talk of their families that I decided on the following Monday, August 22, to visit them in their homes.

Chapter Nine

Up To Johnnycake,
Down to Lick Branch

The scenery along State Rt. 97 is startlingly beautiful. Green hills, mountains covered with tall timber, sparkling streams, pristine valleys. Quiet, too. I travel for miles and not pass another automobile nor see a home. I begin to feel like a corpuscle traveling through a small capillary as I make my way into the heart of the Appalachians.

A few hours later, though, I wind my way up and over busy Johnnycake Mountain, then hold on for dear life as dozens of coal trucks threaten to blow my doors off going down the other side.

At last, I meet up with several generations of the Church family in two locations, first at Bruce's home midway down Johnnycake's steep eastern flank, then at Danny's mobile home on a narrow road clinging to the side of a valley just outside of Iaeger at a place called Lick Branch. The mountains are so steep and the valleys so narrow here that I think they may have to pipe in sunshine.

Here's an excerpt from my interview with Bruce and his wife, Barbara, who is 33.

Barbara: I know they exist, because I've seen them. There for a while it was like every other night.

Bob: When was the last time you saw one?

Barbara: It's been since I moved down here. Like a month or two months ago.

Bob: What'd it look like?

Barbara: It looked like, well, I couldn't see anything but the lights. It looked like there was a glass over top of something, had a light in it. It was a clear night. It was a pretty good long ways away.

Bob: Tell me about the one that means the most to you.

Barbara: The biggest one I saw, it was...I remember seeing it, but I never really paid any attention. So many lights and it was so big and I should have looked for details, but I didn't.

Bob: How big was it?

Barbara: Oh, it was humongous... It was probably last year, year before last. We didn't live here then.

Bob: What'd you think when you saw it?

Barbara: Well, it amazed me. It really shocked me.

I didn't expect to ever see one, but it happened.

I was going to go up to my sister-in-law's. She lived up above me. I was going to get a perm. It was right at the edge of dark. I was walking down the hill and I met Michael, my son. We were down there talking. He just looked up and said, "There's what Dad and I saw." And when I saw that...I don't know, it just flipped me out. It was just non-real to me. And then he ran in the house and left me out in the yard by myself watching that thing. It didn't scare me at the time, but later it did.

Bob: Could it fit on a football field?

Barbara: I can't really say. It was big, it might fit on a football field. But it was kind of more up. It was real high.

(She doesn't recall any unusual thoughts or communications, or any missing time experiences.)

Bob: What do you think these things are?

Barbara: I think they're other people, more advanced than we are.

Bob: Why did you get afraid later?

Barbara: Maybe because I've heard about people being taken up.

Bob: Were you excited?

Barbara: Yes, but I felt calm at the same time. I just wanted everybody to see it. I was amazed, I was yelling for them to come.

Since then, Barbara has seen many, many UFOs.

Bob: Do you feel you were chosen to see them?

Barbara: I've never really thought about it like that. I don't think so. My kids have all seen them. A person at church saw something over her house, twice. His brother, his nephew saw the one he and Michael saw. I've seen them a lot, I don't know if it was 20 times or not.

We saw one one night, out in the yard and it seemed to be coming toward us. And then all of a sudden it disappeared. The night I saw the one set down, they would come through the sky real fast, stop and go in the other direction. Just lights in the sky, no airplane. Stop in midair and go the other way. There were a lot of them.

After lunch at the local restaurant (a former Dairy Queen), we move to Danny's home.

I switch on the recorder and speak with Danny's wife, Betty Church, an assistant manager and billing clerk for a local ambulance service.

Here are excerpts:

Bob: Tell me about the experience with the TV.

Betty: I was playing Super Nintendo. Just me and Candice (their young daughter). Danny was at Bruce's looking for UFOs.

The TV changed channels and there was this roar. It was so loud, it was like— the room was rattling. It wasn't a jet, I could tell a jet. The room was literally shaking. I said, 'Oh—No!'

It scared me— I ran outside. I looked around and over on this mountain, I saw this object. It had different colored lights in it in a diamond shape going around. On the other end it had like red and white lights. Moving real slow and then it was going across the mountain. It went by, on out of sight. It scared me, I called Bruce, but Danny wasn't there, he was outside.

Bob: Did you have an idea what it was?

Betty: Not really at the time. I think it was nothing of our kind. I don't believe it was any of our aircraft. The lights on it were too odd and it didn't, it just glided when it got to the top of the mountain, like it was going to turn. Then it just went out of sight. I never heard the roar anymore when I got outside and saw it.

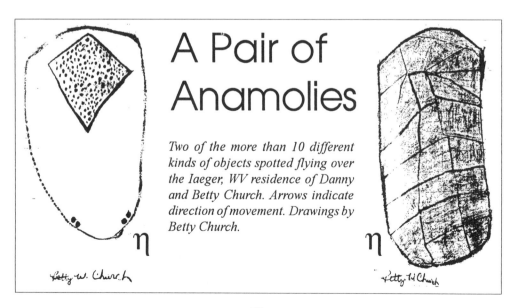

A Pair of Anamolies

Two of the more than 10 different kinds of objects spotted flying over the Iaeger, WV residence of Danny and Betty Church. Arrows indicate direction of movement. Drawings by Betty Church.

Betty said she felt as though "there was somebody on board, steering it," but she didn't know who or what. Interestingly, she could not remember the date or year of the sighting, just as many others I've interviewed could not remember.

More interesting is that her next door neighbor had not heard the roaring noise.

Bob: Why do you think you heard a roar, and your next door neighbor didn't.

Betty: I don't know. I think it's odd.

Danny: That's not the first time. My dad and (someone else) were working on the car here at night. And one went over and Betty saw it. She was trying to yell at them and they couldn't hear her. And they were only maybe 50 feet away.

Betty: I was standing out on the porch and a craft came over. This one was going slow, it was just gliding. I was yelling, 'Look! Look!' But they did not hear me.

Bob: Why?

Betty: I don't know. They were right up here on the next driveway up.

Danny: I was here and saw very little of it. I didn't hear her yelling.

Betty: I was yelling as loud as I could, I was excited. I had opened the door, had my head out the door, just looking around. And when I looked up, it was right over there. It was quiet, there was no sound.

Bob: Why did you poke your head out the door?

Betty: Just looking, I usually do that, just go to the door and look out. That one was shaped like a rectangle, but not a perfect rectangle. The ends were kind of rounded. Maybe like a capsule, but not quite that narrow. The way the lights were under it, the lights ...you know how the lights are on in the house at night and when you're going by how it looks, from the outside? That's what it looked like. All these lights, all under it, covered the whole bottom of it. (See drawing, opposite page.)

It was big. Probably could fit on a football field with not much room left after it landed.

I yelled and yelled, and they couldn't hear me while I was seeing it. After it was gone they heard me fine.

I ask if she has experienced any strange or precognitive dreams. She says no, but the question also elicits a response from Danny.

Danny: I've had this dream about one coming down this valley several times. Same dream every time. Each time it's at night. It comes down out of the north, comes down and sits up in this bottom down here. I haven't seen it yet for real, but it seems like every so often I dream it.

(That leads him into the memory of another sighting.)

It was March 18, my birthday in '93. I left the fire house, coming up to Mom's, they had a cake for me or something. I started up the road right here and I was looking at what looked like a big star. I said, 'I know that's not Jupiter, it's too big.' Looked about the size of a baseball, little bit bigger than a golf ball. I knew it couldn't be a planet or star because it wasn't twinkling. It was just like a light bulb. In the east. I get out of the truck and it's still sitting there. I see some jets come. Two of them, flying together, real close. So I know they're military, that's the only thing that flies together like that. I go inside at Mom's and say, 'You all come outside and look how these planes are flying.' When I came back out, that thing had taken off and outrun those jets, went *ZOOM*—right by 'em. Flew past...

Betty: It looked like it went in between them. It just kept right on going.

Danny: Jets were right behind it and it flew right on past them. Jets weren't going to keep up with something like that. You could hear the jets.

A short while later, the whole mobile home seems full of people, as Danny and Betty are joined by Bruce and Barbara, their son Bruce Jr., Danny's folks and other people I don't know, all gathering like a family reunion after work and coming to see some man from up north who's writing a book about UFOs.

Sometime during the melee, I manage to grab Bruce, Jr. and sit him down at the kitchen table for an interview.

He regards me and my tape recorder warily.

Can't say that I blame him. For one thing, the tie I was wearing had the wildest, brightest pattern on it imaginable, as if it had once been a rag at a paint-spraying contest. Naturally, it had been selected for my ensemble today by the fashion hound in our family, four-year-old Ashley, who had insisted that I wear it, else she would cry.

Bruce David Church, Jr. is "17 going on 18 this month."

Jr: My first experience, was when Mom yelled at me and got me to come out at Garland. We looked up and there's a big space ship going over. You could hardly tell because it was pitch dark. But you could see the lights and it was pretty close. It went up the hill. We looked at it through binoculars, but it was too dark to tell much about it. We watched it go over the hilltop. It didn't make any sound at all.

It was kind of round with rough edges. It was going away from me, just creeping. You could outwalk it.

B: What did you think it was?

Jr: I had my doubts, I did. A lot of doubt about ETs in general. Once I saw that, it opened my eyes. I didn't have any doubts after I saw it. The way it was shaped, the way it was moving, there isn't anything that could do what it did—that we know of. It was humongous.

B: Other sightings?

Jr: I've seen them go faster than my eyes could see. I also saw a couple down in a river. At the time when we first started seeing them, I was playing high school basketball. I get a ride up to the Garland Bridge and then I walk down the tracks that go past the house. Well, it'd take me about 10 minutes to walk down the tracks and then back to the house.

About halfway in the trip, you go around a curve and then down a big long, straight stretch. Right in that curve— there's a big place where everybody swims— there was something. I could see it very well. It spooked me and then I ran.

But at the time I was watching it, it was almost identical to this, a little bit smaller, but almost identical. It had one little detail, I never could understand what it was doing. It had a red, the reddest beam, shooting into

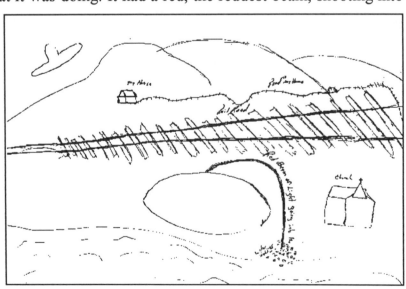

The scene witnessed and later drawn by then 15-year-old Bruce David Church, Jr. as he walked home from playing basketball in 1992.

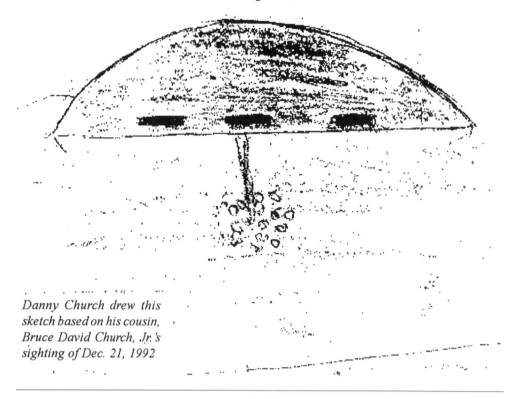

*Danny Church drew this
sketch based on his cousin,
Bruce David Church, Jr.'s
sighting of Dec. 21, 1992*

the water.

I couldn't see the front of it, because there was so much light. I could tell it had hieroglyphics, though.

B: Can you draw those?

Jr: Well, I can't really draw them. I know what they look like but they were in a complex sequence. They're hard to really describe. It's mainly blocks and lines. It wasn't writing like we...like the Indian hieroglyphics.

B: On the outside of this thing?

Jr: Yeah, right on the edges, there wasn't too much light coming from them and I could focus on them before I took off running. I was interested but, it had a beam. Little thing coming down through the water. It was coming off the top, hitting the water.

B: Could you see it go under the water?

Jr: All I could see was it hitting the water. That's all. I started running because it started moving. It scared me to death when it started moving.

B: Did the beam go off when it started moving?

Jr: No, it stayed on when it started, but then it quit. It came down the river towards Iaeger, then it went straight up. It was hard to see, but it went straight up.

Every two to four nights when I would come through, there would be one down there. I don't know what in the world they'd be doing.

B: Did you see other kinds of crafts?

Jr: It was shaped something like an N without the middle bar. Like a half moon. It was thick. It was doing pretty much the same thing only it was, it looked like it was twice the weight. I was right across from it. It had the same beam except it was coming from underneath. It was hitting the water, but this time it was a small, thin, high intensity beam. It looked like it was thinner than paper, very fine. The beam was making a high pitched noise. Like the lasers on Star Trek, something like that, only it was high pitched.

When I first heard it, that's what got my attention. And when I was standing there, you know the first time it scared me, but this time I was more interested in it. I watched it shoot straight up, and once it disconnected that beam, the noise quit. So I do know it was the beam that made the noise.

When it was hitting the water, it was like...glowing, a reddish looking color, shooting out of the water and it

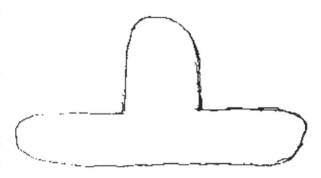

Bruce David Church, Jr.'s drawing of the hat-shaped UFO he saw.

was—you know how a nuclear bomb explodes? A big mushroom cloud, it was like a real mushroom stuff coming out of it. Like it was drilling or something like that. It was bubbling up like a mushroom coming out. I sat there maybe 10 minutes, I didn't want to make a move. I didn't know if they knew I was there or not. They had the same hieroglyphics as the other one. The first one I saw was about 40' away. This one I stood right here at the tracks, and right over there is the creek at the river. I was about that far away from this one. About maybe 20 or 30 feet away.

Bob: Have you experienced lost time?

Jr: No. There was no lapsed time, I wore a watch.

B: Tell me about your most interesting sighting.

Jr: Every time I see them, I see a certain alignment in the stars. It's

Bruce David Church, Jr. relaxes on cousin Danny's deck. Photo by Bob Teets.

like three stars brighter than the stars around them. Very bright. Brighter than the North Star. There's only one time I ever saw anything different than these—when they had three other ones in the center. And that made a complete triangle. They all looked like the same brightness all the way through. (Note: a similar description of star patterns by another youngster who lives at least 150 miles north of Iaeger can be found on Page 164.)

B: Could you see stars around these?

Jr: There were stars around the outside, but there wasn't anything behind the triangle pattern. It was too strange. I thought it was like a mother ship.

Me and Betty (his wife), after Mom and Dad moved over on Johnnycake, were walking home one night. We'd been at Iaeger all day. On the way back, I was looking up and there was about five of them. And one big one, a humongous thing. It looked like it was 600' to 800' high and it looked like a top hat. It consumed the other ones.

It looked like an oval shape.

B: The little one would stop and the big one would come over it?

Jr: No, the big one was sitting still, as plain as day. There were a bunch of little ones flying around, about five of them. They would come from underneath it, almost in the identical place every time. There would be like a....light...came out of the bottom of it, like a door opened to it. It was a clear sky and the moonlight was right there where they were. I've only seen that one time.

B: Any unusual thoughts, like it was trying to communicate with you or anything?

Jr: This one, when I saw it, I thought how good it would be to have a cowboy hat. (laughs) I did have a thought what it would be like to go up there and see what is really up there. How good it would be to go up there and see what that was.

(Note: Following an August cool spell, Danny sent me the following...)

On August 31, 1994 there was an unidentified flying object observed in the Panther area, at Green Brier Mt.—the time was 11 p.m. Two people saw the craft. (Name) states that he first heard what he thought was a

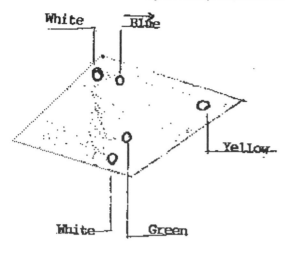

A craft spotted on August 31, 1994 by two people near the Panther State Park. Drawing by Danny Church.

jet, then went outside, but he never saw the plane that he heard. Both people then looked up and saw an object making no noise, and observed it about 15 minutes. The shape was like a diamond, one half of it is all that had lights on it. The colors were yellow, blue, green and white. The white lights were strobe-like in appearance. The other end, which was the back of the craft, did not have any lights on it and was dark in color. The craft was moving very slowly.

Weather: showers to partly cloudy
Temp: 65 degrees

(Obviously, UFO Season has started again in Iaeger.)

A McDowell County Family of UFO Eyewitnesses

The Church Family: (Left) Betty with the family dog. (Below) Candice, Danny, Bruce and Barbara. Photos by Bob Teets.

Chapter Ten

140 Years of UFO History

I had asked via a press release for UFO stories from state residents.

The phone is still ringing, even as I write this two months after the fact. "Bob, the call's for you," has become so standard a sentence at our office that it's now delivered to me in code: "Uf-fo," the wife says. I'm beginning to hear it in my sleep.

Don't get me wrong, I wanted to hear the stories. But I also wanted to write the book by the end of September. This was supposed to be a "quick overview" of West Virginia UFOs. Right.

I never met the vast majority of these people, except through a phone receiver. I regret this fact, since a huge majority of them seemed the sort of people you'd like to know as personal friends. Their stories, in several instances, cried out for on-site visits, but time and money conspired to prevent me from traveling more. Perhaps a sequel, *SON of West Virginia UFOs*—will allow me to do so.

Here, then, in a sort of rough chronological order of event dates (though some follow sequentially as a consequence of being related), is a "quick overview" of the first 140 years of West Virginia UFOs.

1830's

One of the earliest known reports of an anamalous phenomenon occurring in what is now West Virginia happened as Alexander Creel, a passenger on a steamboat plying the Ohio River, happened to look to shore, where he saw an apparition of the Virgin Mary, who told him, "There you behold the site of what will some day be a happy and prosperous city."

Creel purchased the land and later named it St. Mary, which today is St. Marys, West Virginia.[1]

---

1. *West Virginia County Maps,* by C.J. Puetz, County Maps publishers, Lyndon Station, WI

1866

Dr. Mahlon Loomis (1826 - 1886), dentist, scientist and inventor, first demonstrated his two-way wireless communication system between two mountains in nearby Virginia. In subsequent years, he is believed to have perfected his system from three hills in Preston County, West Virginia, where now are located microwave and various radio transmitter antennae, as well as the Etam Earth Station (built in the 1960's to relay radio signals from astronauts in space to Mission Con-

Dr. Mahlon Loomis, inventor of the first "wireless" communication system, is believed to have perfected his invention with the addition of voice signals in Preston County, West Virginia during the 1880's.

trol in Houston, Texas during the early years of America's space program).

Still riding the galactic currents are the Voyager spacecraft launched from earth in 1977 and just now reaching the outer limits of our solar system. On board are greetings from earth citizens to distant cosmic civilizations.

Preceding the Voyager's reach are all radio and television signals ever broadcast from Planet Earth before the spacecraft's launch.

The first modern-age signals, including those of peoples' voices it is said, were propagated by the Loomis system (patented in 1872) and are leading the way.

(For additional information about Dr. Loomis, see Chapter One.)

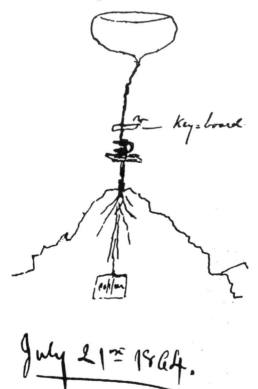

An early sketch of Mahlon's invention, which he drew on his 38th birthday. Images on this page, scanned from, Mahlon Loomis: Inventor of Radio, by Cmdr. (USNR) Thomas Appleby.

1950's

1954 or '55

Charles E. Sisler was nine or ten years old when, in 1954 or 1955, as he was on the way to the outhouse one night, the family dog started whining and looking up at the hillside.

It was a clear night, and the countryside around their farm north of Terra Alta, Preston County, had been quiet.

There, no more than 25 to 30-feet off the ground and no more than 75 to 100 yards away was a craft the "size of a house trailer. I could hear a humming noise. It looked flat almost, and had square windows in it. I could see a yellow glow inside it."

And then, a face, a human being's face, appeared in one of the windows.

"It was like watching a stranger driving by in an automobile," he recalls. "It gave me a weird feeling, that something like that would be going by, because there was no sound except for the humming."

Looking back on it now, he guesses that it may have been a blimp, though they were never reported to travel over this remote and mountainous area of West Virginia, especially after dark and so close to the ground.

The object moved slowly, not

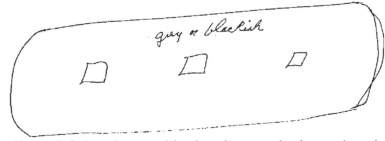

Charles E. Sisler's drawing of the object he saw on his farm in the mid-1950's.

more than 5-10 m.p.h.—"the movement resembled a hot air balloon" floating along—up over the hill and disappeared. "I wasn't really afraid," he says, "because it was moving away from me. Also, the dog would have protected me."

1960's

February, 1960 (Letter Excerpt)

"My mother and I saw what we considered to be a UFO when I was in the 8th grade. There's no fancy story to tell.

"It was seventeen minutes after 4 p.m., February 17, 1960.
"We looked at the skies and hilltops as we ate supper. The length
of time it took me to make a 100-yard dash to the neighbor's
house to get my dad, it had disappeared. We have not seen
anything like it since.

"I did see a fireball cruise the top of the hills where we
lived, but didn't have an identifiable structure. My mother is
still living. I reported my sightings to my school principal and
class. They said it was swamp gas or a weather balloon. They
made fun of me and called me 'nature boy.' So I know how
other people feel.

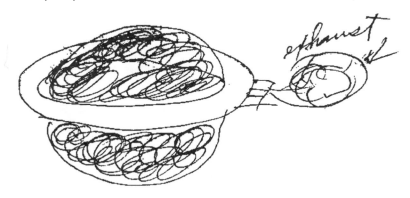

"Center was like solid black or dark grey. Outer ring was
lighter, no lights or other strange features, except for exhaust
ports in back. The exhaust gases looked white or light grey in
color."

Glen Thomas
New Martinsville, WV

1965 or '66

At 11 p.m. one night, Merle Partridge's television "went crazy" with a
high-pitched whine. Then the house lights flickered, their German Shep-
herd Dog out on the front porch started howling at something, and the TV
finally "blew out."

Merle grabbed his 8 mm Mauser rifle and ran outside—

—just in time to see red lights flashing down near the pump house on
their rural Doddridge County farm. Having served in the Air Force, Merle
at first thought it was a helicopter.

The dog howled again and took off for toward the pump house.

"Come back here!" Merle commanded, but the otherwise obedient
dog ignored his master and headed into the darkness.

Merle went back inside to check on the family.

Next morning, the grass nearby the pump house had been mashed down in a curious circular pattern, and the 110-pound dog had disappeared.

A neighbor who lived four miles away contacted Merle and asked him if the Partridge's television had acted funny the night before.

Soon thereafter, Merle and the neighbor grabbed up their guns and searched the area for whatever had caused all the commotion, but they found nothing.

A short while later, Merle heard a report of a large bird standing alongside the road holding the carcass of a big dog.

Things had calmed down a little bit when, a week later, a huge UFO slowly came over the Partridge's swimming pool and "blacked out the sky." Awestruck, the family watched the giant craft that looked to Merle as if it had been "put together with metal plates and bolts," (which years later he thought resembled the construction of the craft featured on the television program, "Battlestar Gallactica.")

Then, two or three nights later, Merle heard pounding on his front door. "I need help!" some man yelled from outside.

Recent events had caused the Partridge family to be "highly spooked at the time," so anything unusual was likely to be put to a severe test. "'You sure do!'" Merle, holding his Mauser, called back to whomever was on the porch, "'Cause I'm going to blow a hole through the door in about a minute.'"

His decency overcame his fear, however, so he opened the door to see a man and a young boy standing on the porch. They both looked shell-shocked and frantic.

Seems the man had wrecked his car after seeing a UFO, and by the time the man had wrested himself and one son free of the car, the other son who had also been a passenger in the car was nowhere to be found.

Merle and the man hopped in Merle's pickup and sped off north, toward the scene of the accident. They travelled about a quarter mile to where the man's car was lying in a ditch. Using flashlights and the headlights of Merle's truck, they searched the vicinity for the missing boy, but without success. They then hooked a chain to the car and pulled it out of the ditch.

Heading back toward the house, with the man following in his car, Merle saw a kid walking from the opposite direction.

The man stopped his car, hopped out and hugged the boy. Curiously, the boy seemed to have no response to his father's ministrations.

To Merle, the boy appeared to be physically unharmed, but shell-shocked. Reportedly, the boy had no memory of how he had gotten so far away from the scene of the crash in so short a time.

Merle recalls now that a subsequent investigation by personnel from Wright-Patterson Air Force base in nearby Ohio (probably members of "Project Blue Book," which the Air Force closed down in 1969) "tried to make us look like fools."

The families involved also suffered a "lot of ridicule" and received numerous crank calls, where a voice on the other end of the line would say, "*Coo-coo! coo-coo!*"

"At that time I was classed as an idiot," Merle says.

But that didn't change Merle's mind.

"I know what I saw," he asserts, "they can yell 'swamp gas' or whatever they want, but I know what I saw.

"After the incident with the dog, for two weeks it was the weirdest, eeriest thing around where we lived. It was too quiet. You'd see birds, but they wouldn't be singing. Our farm animals were spooked like I'd never seen them. There were no crickets or frogs at night. It was just like you had stuck plugs in your ears. We considered moving away."

One day many years after the events, a man with a beard walked up to Merle and introduced himself as the boy who had temporarily disappeared that night back in the 60's, Merle says. They talked about what had happened, but they both remained mystified by the whole ordeal.

Now, however, and with years to think about it, Merle says, "It's not scary to me anymore. We're not the only beings in the universe. Now, call me an atheist or what you want. My own conclusion is that there are beings much smarter than us, and if we met them, we may think of them as God. Of course, everybody is entitled to their own opinion."

Merle currently lives with his wife in New Martinsville. They have six children and 18 grandchildren.

October, 1966 (and July, 1994, sort of)

This story actually starts and ends in 1994, when, on July 7, I received a call from Linda Nippert.

"A UFO landed here many years ago," Linda said, "and I heard that aliens or something had walked through the house I now live in."

(Linda, 56, knows about such things. One time, when she was 16 or so, she accompanied her father and some others on a trip to deliver lumber. The group was forever mystified when they later discovered that the trip had taken two hours longer than they could account for.)

Linda said she, her daughter and son-in-law bought the place a little over a year ago and that's when neighbors told her about the UFO landing and a spot down in the woods where nothing would grow.

While telling me this story, she indicated that the man who used to own the house was a lawyer, but that was all she knew.

We immediately brought to bear the maximum resources of our vast publishing empire in order to locate the individuals. (Actually, my wife called the Tyler County courthouse and found Mrs. Berry's name in about two minutes.)

Mrs. O. G. Berry was awakened by the sound of footsteps as some-one or some*thing* was walking from the reception hall to the front room on the first floor of their three-story Victorian house in Middlebourne, Tyler County. It was October, 1966.

"I was frightened," Mrs. Berry recalls, "I knew something was wrong."
Then, she realized the sound seemed to be coming from the back porch.
"I reached over and touched my husband, so I knew it wasn't him."
Whatever it was seemed to walk back and forth, back and forth.
"All at once I heard a motor start," but she never heard a car leave.

The next morning, her husband, a successful lawyer, was reading the paper during breakfast, and happened to look out the window where he spied a curious black spot down in the woods.

The next door neighbor a short time later also noticed the spot, and told Mrs. Berry that she, too, had heard someone walking on the Berry's porch, around 4 a.m. In addition, she said she had heard an odd noise, like the swishing sound made when closing a refrigerator door.

There had been no frost so far that year, Mrs. Berry recalls, and yet an inspection of the spot revealed that all grass and weeds, "some as high or three or feet," and trees within the 40-foot circular spot "crumbled to the ground like ashes. It was peculiar, that spot was black as could be, but it didn't look charred."

Two weeks later, she says, many people in the area reported seeing UFO's.

She and her husband (who is now deceased) were reluctant to report their findings at the time, she says, because they feared it may adversely affect his law practice.

"The imprint could be seen for three years," she later wrote in a letter sent to me. "She (Mrs. Berry's neighbor) and I talked about the motor starting and never hearing a movement of any kind. Why was someone on the porch, did he stop, trying to get a better view? Why were my neighbor and I afraid to get up and look from our windows? I'm afraid we will never have an answer.

"I lived there eight years after my husband died, too much house for one person, so I moved."

(Note: Mrs. Berry also reports that she and her family were vacationing on the Florida coast around 1968 or so. At a restaurant one evening, her husband called their son outside to watch an amazing display of lights in the sky. Soon, many people from the restaurant and along the shoreline were gawking at the lights, which Mrs. Berry described as resembling the construction of "old Model T Ford headlights, with the little grooves in them." But these lights did not appear to be fastened to anything, she recalls, even though the people watching had looked at them through binoculars. Just as the show was getting good, U.S. military jets screamed into the area and "these lights disappeared in a flash," she says. *This took place in a quaint tourist town named Destin, located only a short drive from the famed 1980's UFO hot spot known as Gulf Breeze.*)

And now back to the rest of Linda's story.

"My dog won't stay on the main floor nor in one other room in particular, the master bedroom," she told me.

"Do you think it's connected to the story about aliens walking through the house?" I ask.

"I don't know," she replies, "but it sure could be."

1968

It was four days before Thanksgiving, and the Southall family was already preparing for the big day at their home out on Southall Ridge, beyond Ripley.

Sixteen-year-old Eathel Southall and his 14-year-old cousin were in the front yard on the beautiful evening killing a turkey for the feast to come.

Suddenly, the family dog became agitated, and Eathel followed its stares upward, just as a large object—"the biggest thing I ever saw, at least 50 yards in diameter, with red, blue, green and amber lights— flew right over our house and landed some distance away in an old, overgrown field, decimating everything in its path, including trees." Then, "It seemed like it started shooting pods of some sort up into the sky."

Before Eathel could stop his cousin, the other boy had grabbed a .22 rifle and had begun firing away.

His aim must have been true, for when the first bullet hit the craft, "it went—*whomp*," Eathel recalls. But there didn't appear to be any damage.

Eathel Southall's drawing of his family's sighting in 1968.

Subsequent shots missed, he says, because, despite its size, the craft seemed agile enough to dart one way or the other and avoid the shells.

Meanwhile, Helen Southall, Eathel's mother, was out in the back yard with other members of the family.

"We started noticing these things popping up and down in midair," she states. "They were round and lighted and popping up to about the height an airplane would be allowed to fly at low altitude. They looked like beacons, not real bright, but like a dome that would go up and go around in a circle."

A daughter recalls an object "hovering over the neighbor's field" and "beams of light falling down to the ground. Mom called the Kanawha County airport and told them about it." She doesn't remember seeing anything on the ground.

"I don't like those things!" she exclaims now.

Because of their position, those in the back yard couldn't see anything like a large craft sitting in the old field across from the front of the house.

But Eathel and his cousin watched as the big ship eventually lifted out of the woods and disappeared slowly over the hills toward Ripley.

"I still look for them, I still believe in them," Eathel, now 42, says. He remembers writing a report about the event for his social studies class.

Helen, his mother, says she always carries a camera with her now. "We call them UFOs today," she states, "but they're in the Bible. Things can appear, can happen for a reason. It can be a warning, or it can bring good news. There are going to be great things happening! People are going to be saying, 'What an awesome God we've got!'"

Late 1960's - 1994

Pete Z. (not his real name) and his wife were travelling home late one night in 1967 or '68 when they spotted a bright light "not as big as the moon, but much bigger than a star" moving southward across their line of sight.

Pete started "acting a fool with my wife" and teasing her about signalling whatever it was flying by. As a result, he switched the headlights off and on four or five times.

Much to the couples' surprise, the object stopped in midair, "then came over top of the car."

Pete sped up, but the object remained overhead—for 30 miles!

He was scared, he says, and his wife was crying.

When they finally reached home, he sent his wife inside to be with their children while he remained outside to keep an eye on the object, still high overhead.

Finally, it left "in a flash," Pete says.

But that was just the beginning.

Four or five months later, Pete had worked a double shift at the mines, so had cleaned up and gone to bed for some sound sleep.

After repeated attempts sometime later, his wife finally awakened him.

"There was a high-pitched sound in the room," Pete says, "and shadows being cast across the bedroom from a light shining through the window."

He rushed to the window and threw open the curtains—

—just in time to see an object shoot off into the night with a "50-foot trail of fire behind it."

Pete isn't sure of a date, but sometime after these events, he and members of the family lay on a blanket one summer night and watched "a large light with smaller ones coming out of it" put on a "show" that lasted for over two hours. The lights, Pete states, "would zigzag, shoot off and make 90-degree turns, you name it."

And then, sometime during all of these sightings, Pete had a visitor one night.

He was working on a project at his workbench in the basement when he sensed his wife standing behind him.

"I can't stand having anybody behind me," he says, "so I whirled around to scold her, and— it was the awfulest looking thing..."

Standing a few feet away from him was a green, 5-foot tall, rough-skinned reptilian-looking creature with "bug eyes, lips an inch thick and great long arms. It must have weighed 200 pounds," Pete says, "and I thought, 'Oh, my God, it's blocking the door!'

"It didn't blink or anything. It had bug eyes as big as the bottom of a drinking glass. I about had a heart attack."

Before Pete could come up with a plan of action, though, "It left, it just disappeared," he says.

When he ran upstairs, his wife looked at him and said, "You're white as a sheet! What's wrong?"

Pete then told her what had happened. As he thought about it later, though, he says he wondered if perhaps he had imagined the creature. And yet, the details of its appearance had been so vivid.

"Maybe, just maybe it was something from outer space," he says.

Pete now reads a lot about UFOs and such, though neither he nor his wife have had any other close-up sightings or experiences since that time in the late 60's and through the 70's.

He adds, however, that "I get a feeling once in a while, I can feel it. I go outside and I can see it, high up in sky."

1970's

February 7, 1970

Glenda R. Moore was expecting her fifth child when, on this day, her other four children and a neighbor kid were playing outside in the family's New Martinsville yard. Suddenly, 14-year-old daughter Amy ran down into the basement where Glenda was doing laundry— "Come quick!" the girl yelled.

When Glenda reached the kitchen, she looked out the window and "saw a space ship hovering over the neighbor's house!"

Her immediate thought was, "They're after my kids!"

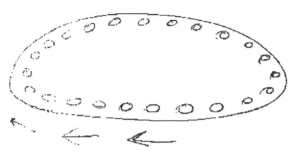

Her husband was in Texas at the time, so she rushed all the children into the car and drove into town where the family's steel fabricating plant was located. There, in the presence of steelworkers, she felt safe. No more had she arrived, though, when two U.S. military jets flew overhead and streaked into the distance, as if giving chase to the UFO.

Glenda Moore's hand-drawn image of what she saw in 1970.

"It was like it was observing us," she recalls now. "And I wondered who they wanted, me, because I was pregnant, or the kids. It was round, bowl-shaped on top, and looked pinched together around the edges like a pie. Its lights rotated counterclockwise."

Amy (now Amy Moon) remembers the ship was silver, oval-shaped, and had lights around the bottom. It was silent while it hovered. "In the blink of an eye, it disappeared," she says. "Then the jets came."

Amy had other sightings, too, back in the 60's when she was eight or nine. Since that time, she says, her psychic abilities, what she calls her "second sense," have continually increased. She says her father also possesses similar abilities, though he doesn't pay much attention to it.

Amy now has five children of her own, aged 11 to 21, and lives in Pasa Robles, California, where she is an office manager for a small service company. Her husband manages a plant that makes computer parts.

"I felt like they were watching us," she says of the 1970 sighting. "I felt like there were many aboard."

Glenda and her husband, John "Jerry" Moore, reside in Texas, though she would like to return to West Virginia. She says another of her daughters is now involved in a UFO group close to Houston because some of her experiences "bugged her thoughts."

1966 - 1977

June Platter lives in Grafton, WV, where's she seen at least three UFOs. Her first sighting occurred, she says, in 1966, when neighborhood dogs "were going nuts." She and her mother looked from their hillside home across to the Tygart Dam, located about a half-mile away. There, hovering over the dam, was a cigar-shaped UFO. "It looked like an airplane with no wings," she says. "No tail, rudder, it wasn't pointed like an airplane." Even from that distance, the women could "hear a humming sound, like when you're standing under electric wires."

June remembers: "I said, 'Oh! My word, look at that!' I wasn't afraid, but I was excited. Awestruck. I thought, 'I bet there's energy in that dam, and that's what they're doing, taking energy.'"

Then—the craft shot "off in a flash, straight away from us," and disappeared.

Even though her mother had shared in the sighting, June recalls, the woman would never discuss it because of her religious beliefs.

Her second sighting took place in 1976 or '77.

She used to go into work early at the "Sandwich Shop," a restaurant in town, to prepare the day's fare. On this particular morning, she had stopped by to pick up a co-worker between 5 and 5:15 a.m.

She noticed a "very bright star" overhead, and pointed it out to her co-worker, who was just entering the car. "I said, 'What is that?' And she answered, 'I never saw a star shaped like that.'"

"It was shaped like a football, and seemed so close that you could almost reach out and touch it."

The women proceeded on to work, but when the co-worker's father went outside of his home 20-minutes later, the "star" had disappeared.

June's third sighting was one of the most odd UFO stories I've heard, and though I had no reason to disbelieve her, it was strengthened when I later heard a nearly identical story from an independent source over 200 miles away. First, June's experience.

June, her two daughters (aged 29 and 25) and another female, a 25-year-old friend of the daughters', were returning from a shopping trip one evening. (I didn't get the date.)

"Look," one of the girls said, "there's another gas well."

Given that a number of wells were in the area, June would hardly have paid any attention, except that this appeared to be a new one and was quite large, judging by the height and size of the drilling rig and the rows of lights climbing its drill tower. "Boy, that's a big one," she replied.

Suddenly—

"It took off and flew in behind us and cars behind us!" June exclaimed. "I thought, 'Buddy, if you're going to cart me off, I want to see you first!'— so I jumped out of my car."

Others did, too.

June suddenly had the sensation that her chest was being squeezed.

"The man behind us said, 'Boy, I'm glad I live right.' And I said, 'Maybe we're all seeing things.'"

Soon, the whole thing just "disappeared in a flash," June said.

I asked her, during our interview, if she saw any significance to her having seen three separate UFOs, while most people never see one.

"I don't see any significance," she responded. "I think there's lot of people who see them and absolutely don't say a word about it."

More than a month after my phone interview with June, I had travelled to Southern West Virginia, where I met up with the Church family (see their stories, beginning on Page 63.)

It was Danny Church who relayed to me the story of his having talked with an older woman somewhere near Iaeger who had noticed some odd lights against a far mountain one night when she was looking out her window. She knew full well that no road existed on that section of the mountain, so the possibility of seeing such bright lights seemed impossible.

She later phoned a few neighbors, and before long a sizeable group of people had gathered, some with binoculars and cameras, as they began a sort of vigil.

Many in the group began to speculate that, because of the general appearance of the lighted apparatus, perhaps a gas well was going in, a hopeful sign to an area where so many people were out of work.

Then, all of the sudden, the "whole thing took off like a space shuttle launch," Danny said the woman told him.

Another unexplained phenomenon. Another busted hope.

And a pair of nearly identical stories from two areas of the state.

1960's - 1990's

Earl Wayne Menefee says he's never served in the armed forces, but his military-like style in crisply reporting 30 years' worth of sightings in and around the Farmington (Marion County) area reminds me of a soldier's diary.

Earl claims he may write a book someday about his experiences, so he ask that I copyright his stories in his name.

April or May, 8th Grade, 1967
Four objects pass in 20-minute span of time. Clear or mostly clear sky after 7:00 p.m. Observed for a couple of minutes.

9th Grade, April of 1968
Good Friday, Easter Weekend
Between 2:00 and 2:30 p.m., clear or mostly clear sky. Observed for a few minutes.
Silver disc hovered or seemed to. Turned on steep bank to port side almost a 90° angle.

10th Grade, September, 1968
About 7:10 p.m. Observed for a minute or less.
Object flew south behind hill. Vehicle covered in mist or fog, then leading edge mist cleared and a little mist cleared at bottom. Lights did not pulsate or blink. Red light in center bottom.

Red light

The next series of UFO sightings took place between October 1971 to December 1971 and/or early 1971.

I would be walking down Chatham Hill toward Farmington to church on Wednesday evenings between 6 and 7 p.m. I saw a white, flashing or strobing light. It wasn't far but there was no engine, rotor, etc. sound, totally quiet.

It was dusk with some light and I could make out no silhouette of a larger craft. It followed a parallel path or course to me, only it was over the ridge across Buffalo Creek. I'd say it was a drone probe. It paralleled me six to eight weeks in a row always on Wednesday evenings walking to church.

This next sighting occurred on Friday October 11, 1974. It was between 8:30 and 9 p.m. or after. Took place in woods area behind where I live. Red line to the naked eye, but with 7 x 50 power binoculars, I could see four red

94

lights around presumed circumference. Presumed disc-shaped object. Object moved slowly, treetop level, as if "searching" for something.

Was at some distance but no engine noise detected. Clear night.

The next sighting occurred late summer or early fall of 1974.
The woods back of where I live on the "far-ridge."
To the west a single, steady glowing, red light hovering behind and above pasture hill. It faced West Farmington area. It hovered for a few minutes then dropped on a down and forward "J"-shaped arc. It was then below the top of the hill.

Opinion: red light drone probe released by disc, "scout," red, craft.

Opinion: it ducked down to keep from being observed.

Within a minute or so of observing this object, I saw another, separate, object.

Disc-shaped.
Dull red glow over and/or encompassing object. No strobes of any kind. Relatively close, but no engine noise. Down below tops of hills. Clear night.

The next sighting occurred in April of 1976. I would say it was Thursday, April 15.

It was up North (Rt.) 250, out on "East Run Road" not far from the "Four States" intersection. It was near a friend's farm.

Four white lights on presumed circumference of craft. Port side light slightly brighter than other three. It hovered silently for several minutes. It was a clear, starry night, probably after 9 p.m.

Object hovered on slight cant angle as shown and observed with naked, unaided eye. Object about size as shown. Note that it is same type as observed on Friday, October 11, 1974 except lights are white instead of red.

Coincidence, object there or, it followed me?

These last two major sightings occurred in January and February 1990.

The first sighting of object may have been on Saturday January 27. Uncertain of date but was on same day that meteor was videotaped by Salem man. Meteor burned about 17-20 seconds or so. About 34,000 feet.

Short, round "fuselage" section at rear. No tail fins of any kind. Front.

Chrome or Metallic Silver like spoon. Object silent, no engine noise.

May have had slight curvature on top surface but bottom pronoucedly curved like spoon, ladle, pelican beak. Angle of climb shallow, about as shown.

January sighting probably between 5:30 to 5:45 p.m.

Observed for 1 or 2 minutes.

February 1990 sighting of same object. Uncertain as to date but was also on a Saturday, 5:20 p.m.

Both sightings about dusk, but good light level.

On sighting of object I ran upstairs to get camera. It took me about one minute.

Object was gone.

Both times object moved slowly. The second time while getting my camera object must have "punched it." I ran outside and it was gone. It wasn't visible in any of four directions nor straight up overhead.

It cloaked, interphased, or interwarped, or put on an incredible burst of speed. Anybody's guess!

For the rest of this report I want to cover some sundry odd other sightings that were made by others in my area that I accept as credible, unofficially.

I also saw a steady shining, red light make a slow right angle turn in the early to mid-seventies.

A mother and her son down near Farmington and another teenage boy at that time on two different occasions saw the white, flashing, strobing light that I saw.

Back around the later 1940's or early 1950's, two credible witnesses, one of whom is now deceased, saw a tall "man" walking up our street on Chatham Hill while she was waiting for her husband to get home from afternoon shift in the mines. It may have been between 11:30 p.m. and 12:00 a.m.

"It" had a long, shiny green "robe" on and a red "cap" on its head. Its head was up under the old street light flange. That put it at about 12 to 15 feet tall.

The two women were frightened, of course, and ran into their houses.

This next sighting occurred on Friday evening December 20, 1974. It was about 6 p.m. or so, if memory serves me right.

Red lights, steady shine, no engine noise. One light came up after the other vertically, then took off faster than a helicopter in three different directions.

Position of red lights after ascent. Vertical position one above the other ascended then took off at high speed in different direction.

← Position of red lights after ascent. vertical position one above the other ascended then took off at high speed in different directions.

Objects, light, first spotted over Chatham Hill ball field by two teenage boys. By the excited tone of voice as I immediately spoke to them, they seemed sincere.

This next sighting takes place in late 1960's to 1971.

100 to 200 feet across. Deep or dark amber colored light on bottom. Two rows of small, blue lights, possibly about circumference.

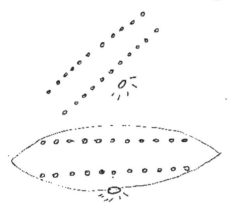

Suggested shape of object (bottom drawing)?

At first in sky just looked like star. Came down on slanted angle, barely cleared knoll, in wood, valley back of houses.

Witness stepped half out of car to make certain no light reflections optical illusions created by car window, windshield, etc. Went downtown to store, came back up to top of Chatham Hill where first saw.

Second time saw two white lights come up onto sky and take off horizontally in two different directions.

(Suggest white lights drone, probe. Keep watch for mothership until repairs, business, whatever finished.)

Witness believes perhaps repairs because of steep angle of descent. He thought of rounding some of us up to go back and take a look but didn't, for he feared for our safety.

The next day witness's wife and her friend saw round craft UFO, disc, whatever up in sky. The UFO formed a "cloud" around itself and disappeared into the other clouds.

Same witness and wife in 1970's also saw one on an evening in June? What appeared to be evening star or Venus but after awhile took off at high speed to the east.

I want to finally cover a couple of incidents of my own. It was autumn or early winter of 1975 or 1976? I was walking to work one morning. It was cold, clear and starry after 6 a.m. I looked behind me when I was near Farmington. I saw a "star" following me. I stopped dead still from walking, turned my head and looked behind me. I saw forward movement or momentum to the "star" for just a second or two. It did not fool me. It was no natural star, it was a UFO.

On a few occasions from my house I have observed across Buffalo Creek on the other ridge a red light moving east to west, or west to east, slowly.

One night, keeping my eyes "locked" onto the red, steady glowing light, I actually saw it change direction from going east to west to moving back towards the east. It moved slowly.

When it changed direction it made no turn, banking maneuver, loop-up or down, or no other standard maneuver. It moved, stopped, headed back.

Over the same ridge and area from my house I have several times observed a white light(s) or "star" that shined steadily. It will dim and brighten at times as if to throw me off and discourage me from viewing it or to gain attention.

Whenever conventional aircraft, airplanes, etc. come near it, it dims down or goes completely black.

As soon as the airplane, etc. passes, the object comes back up to full or partial brilliance. (It doesn't want the other pilots to see it, in my opinion.)

On one night a friend of mine observed this type of object and dim to bright phenomenon with me.

It would seem, Bob, that we are being observed.

Reminiscent of the "Star Trek: The Next Generation" episode *Who Watches The Watchers.*

Easter Sunday, 1973

Like June Platter (see story on previous pages), Kathy McWilliams lived in Grafton during the 1970's. Her story is similar to June's first sighting, but the possible implications are far more disturbing.

It was Easter Sunday, 1973, "a real warm evening," Kathy says.

Her father had been the first to notice. "Look at that out there," he had said, pointing from their hillside home toward the Tygart Dam across the valley, "I thought it was a star or something, but it's not."

Kathy thought it looked like "something was rotating, red and green lights, then lights coming up out of it. It was fantastic."

The family still talks about watching "the aerial display" that lasted over three hours that evening. "At some point," Kathy recalls, "there was a light that came down low and fast over our head—no noise at all—and went over and joined the others at the dam.

"I have not doubted UFOs since that time," she tells me. "I felt that there were occupants on board that craft or ship, and that they were intelligent." They didn't try to communicate with her, or were not there "for me personally," she adds.

But then, she begins talking about losing the baby.

"I never had connected the UFO sighting with the loss of the baby until I thought about calling you," she tells me on the phone. "I have connected it now, because you know how you connect dates with events in your life."

The day after Easter in 1973, she had gone to a doctor in Phillipi, who immediately placed her in a hospital. She was hemorrhaging.

"You're pregnant, and you're losing it," he told her. The next day, she had a D&E, but is unsure if she had lost the fetus prior to the procedure.

"I have had psychic, paranormal experiences since then," she says, "but I can't remember if I had any before then. I do have a lot of those types of dreams. They are like symbols. Eerie. It used to bother me, but now I just accept it."

In response to one of my questions, she says, "I can't recall any sightings with the death of my second baby," a male that died shortly after birth two years later, on August 8, 1974.

Eventually, however, she did successfully give birth to a girl, who is now 18. Her story is next.

Spring, 1991

Eighteen-year-old Katy once lived with an aunt in Grafton for the period of about a year, from sometime in 1990 until July of 1991. Katy was 15 at the time.

"I used to sleep walk a lot when I stayed there for some reason," she says. "I once tracked weeds into the house. And another time, I woke up at Indian Rock, about a quarter mile away" from her aunt's place.

One night, however, she woke up in bed and noticed the lights were on in her room. "I thought it was a dream at first," she says, "because I couldn't roll over, I was on my back. I couldn't move."

But as she glanced sideways, she noticed there were no corners in the room.

"I felt a buzzing in my right ear, and I could feel something on my neck. That's when I knew I was awake."

One part of her was afraid, but she "felt another presence beside me that kept me from moving, even though the bed seemed to be moving. The presence made me feel calm."

She continued lying on the bed for about ten minutes. Then, abruptly, "my body jerked and I saw the door shut and the lights dimmed."

Terrified, she eventually got the "courage to check the whole house," only to find that both exterior doors had been locked from the inside.

"I've tried to explain it away, but it still makes me uncomfortable," she acknowledges. "And I still have déja vu a lot. My dreams go in cycles of the precognitive type. I've always done that a lot."

Fall, 1973 and Spring, 1994

Mickel Q. (not his real name), a college student in Kentucky, calls me July 12, 1994, to report that six or seven rings from 10- to 90-feet in diameter and aligned east/west have been seen in his grandmother's fields for a long time. "A new one formed last week," he adds. "I also saw a blue light there, too" he adds.

We discuss this for a while, when Mickel finally suggests that his mother join in the conversation.

The next voice I hear on the line is that of Jenny Q. (not her real name) who has two stories to tell.

In 1973, Jenny was driving her boys, Mickel (16 ½-months-old at the time), Jonathan (9), and Stanley (6), along a road near the State Police barracks in Ripley, when she suddenly noticed an orange, 15' triangular craft with white tips "fluttering" close by.

It emitted a humming sound, and began following Jenny's car. She pulled off to observe the craft—that is, until it came to within 20 or 25 feet of the car, at which time she felt "shivers running up my back, and a feeling like it was going to try to swoop down and take us."

The next thing she remembers is seeing the craft "flutter around for a short while, then make a straight line up the valley," where it disappeared.

Inexplicably, she could not account for approximately 10 minutes of the time she was in view of the craft.

Her second sighting was just as puzzling.

A neighbor called her one night in 1989 and said the woods on a nearby hill were "on fire."

Jenny looked out her window and could see no fire, but she continued watching— for the next *seven* hours.

She could see a "huge light," which would "open its mouth," reminding her of the Pac-Man game, and emit a smaller light, which in turn would shoot quickly upwards at great speed and in a straight line to a height of about a quarter mile. This it did seven times, she recalls.

Stanley, who was then in his 20's and living at home, watched the spectacle, too, but eventually tired of it and went to bed, she says.

She knows that neighbors were watching it, too. At one point, a neighbor called and tried to get her to call the sheriff. But Jenny didn't do so.

"Why did you watch it for seven hours?" I ask.

"I wanted to watch it until it disappeared," she responds, "because it was something that I didn't trust."

Before we finish our interview, Jenny mentions one more thing. Stanley, her son, has a brown, 1¼-inch birthmark—in the shape of a perfect triangle— on him.

1972 or '73

Ruth Yeager is a special person, at least to UFO buffs. Up until recently, this librarian worked at cataloging and preserving the Gray Barker Collection, presented to the Clarksburg Library in the recent past. Barker, a West Virginian and "one of ufology's most controversial authors," according to *UFO Magazine*, died in 1984.

Ruth has more than a vocational interest in UFOs and its various authors, however.

She has a sighting in her memory.

It was 1972 or '73 when Ruth and her husband were driving along Interstate 64 outside of Huntington. Off in the distance, across some open farmland, "we spotted four to six lights flipping around" in a crazy pattern. "They were zipping around at forty-five and ninety-degree angles," she states, "so we pulled off the Interstate and watched them for maybe 15 minutes."

The couple was too far away from the objects to make out a shape, but Ruth knew they weren't helicopters or any conventional aircraft. "It was awe-inspiring," she recalls, and believes the objects were "intelligently driven crafts" of some type, "not of this earth."

The sighting didn't change her life or anything, she says, "because I've always believed in life in outer space."

1975 (Letter Excerpt):

July 18, 1994
One night in the fall of 1975 while coming home from Masontown, we saw a big red ball of light in the northeast sky and thought the neighbor's house was on fire. We went to where we thought it would be, but as we got near it, the lights on our truck went out then back on. We turned around and the same thing happened again in the same place. We could still see the big red ball of light.

It was a weird feeling.

My husband wanted to go home and get the car, but I said no, because the boys didn't know where we were, and if something happened to us, no one would know.

The next day nothing was on the radio, and nobody else said anything about the big red ball of light.

We talk about it.

Mrs. Beckie Wagner

1974 (+-)

Cameron, West Virginia, resident Janet Deegan taught high school English in Marshall County, so words came easily to mind one night when she was travelling home after visiting her mother in a Wheeling hospital.

She had watched a bright light in the sky for some time when she came to a fork in Route 250 at Poplar Springs.

Not long afterward, she noticed she had a traveling companion, so she slowed down in order to have a good look at it.

No more than 100 feet away and perhaps 50 to 60 feet above the ground was "a typically round, pulsating, saucer" mimicking her car's every movement. "When I would come to a turn," it would make the same maneuver she did, "and it maintained a speed identical to mine," she says now, remembering that night. "Evidently, it was observing me. I was delighted to see it! I wanted to examine it. I was not afraid of it at all."

She definitely had a sense that there were occupants inside the hull of the craft, which she estimated to be about 25 feet in diameter. She could see an alternating yellow/red glow coming through what she called the "portholes" along the craft's exterior.

It followed her until she came to a high school football field in Clausen, and then it proceeded on up the valley while she began her ascent of Cemetery Hill. By the time Janet arrived back in Cameron, it was too late to

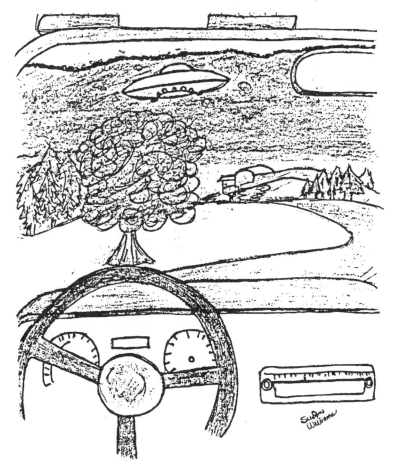

West Virginia artist Susan Williams interprets Janet Deegan's mid-1970's sighting.

share her story with anyone.

"But I told my students at school the next day!" she exclaimed.

1972

Pilot P.E. Carpenter and a friend were making their first pass over the airport at Weston/Jane Lew, checking for other air traffic in the vicinity before setting down.

His friend called his attention to the southwest, where they both then spotted a spherical, shiny object aloft.

His friend continued watching while Carpenter glanced away.

"Look, it's gone," the friend said.

Sure enough, the sphere had disappeared from sight.

On another occasion, this time while on the ground, Carpenter was waiting one evening for the sky to darken so he could observe the heavens through his telescope.

He suddenly spotted a fuzzy, orange/yellow disc coming out of the west.

"I did manage to put the scope on it," he tells me during his call, "but the disc still looked fuzzy, even though the telescope was in focus." The reason, he explains, is that the object must have been a very long distance away and his scope wasn't powerful enough to give a sharp, magnified image.

The disc "continued in a straight line unlike "space junk" he had watched that would describe an arc as it followed the curvature of the earth, with constant speed and track," he says.

"I am not a UFO buff," he adds with a scoff.

After those experiences, I wouldn't know why not.

1978 - '79

Louie Belcastro, an A&P grocery store manager, was crossing the Virginia/West Virginia state line on I-64 headed towards White Sulphur Springs, WV, one night when he had to answer nature's call.

He exited on Rt. 220, a familiar road to him, and drove a short distance before he rounded a turn and spied a pull-off on the left. It was late, and there was no traffic, so he steered the car into the spot, got out and took care took of business.

After finishing, he was about to enter his car when he looked down the road about 60 or 70 yards, near the turn he had just passed a few minutes before. At first, he thought a fire had suddenly erupted a short distance off the road in the woods. But, even after switching off his tail-lights, which he thought may have been casting a reflection to the spot, he could see that the intense red light was something else.

He couldn't believe his eyes. It appeared to an eight-foot tall, two-foot round cylindrical pipe of some type, glowing bright red and reminding him of a fire plug or a stovepipe.

"It was beautiful in a way," he remembers. "It glistened, like red-hot."

But it was scary, too. The object emitted no sound, and seemed to have come out of thin air.

He watched it for about a minute, then got back in the car, rolled up the windows, locked the doors and cautiously backed the car down the road to the spot.

"It was gone," he says now, recalling that night. "I slowly, and I mean slowly, got out and checked around, but I couldn't see a thing."

The next day while listening to a CBS news broadcast out of New York, Louie was shocked to hear that more than 200 UFO sightings had been reported the night before from the area where he had been.

Later, some of Louie's friends in Hinton and Talcott told him of their watching strange lights flying around on the horizon that same night.

"I thought afterwards that it, whatever it was, was connected with an intelligence of some sort," he says.

October, 1977

Twenty-one-year-old Gloria (not her real name), her younger sister and two other girlfriends were headed down a rural Wetzel County road near Mobley about 8:30 p.m. one evening in the Fall of 1977.

Gloria, who was driving, glanced up in the sky and noticed what she thought at first was a helicopter gliding down over the road in front of her car no more than 80 yards away.

Then she knew it was no helicopter. "I was in total awe. It sort of looked like a metallic, silvery hat with red and blue flashing lights," she says. "It was larger than the car."

Then the car radio quit.

Gloria steered the car onto the side of the road and, with the engine still running, watched the mysterious craft "glide down onto a point on a hill into some trees. The whole top of the hillside looked like the glow you see at night coming from a lighted football field."

She remembers "tears running down my cheeks that I didn't put there."

Her next thought was, "Let's get out of here!"

Quickly, she drove across a small bridge onto the North Fork Road, and, looking back, she saw the light "moving incredibly fast upward in a Z pattern." It quickly disappeared.

Later, and even accounting for the time they watched the craft, the foursome couldn't account for 30 minutes of their trip. One of the girls, who was in the front seat with Gloria, broke out in a rash for two days. Gloria had strange recurring dreams for a short while in which she saw herself "standing in a field beside a UFO with steps coming down."

And now, 38-year-old Gloria is still mystified by the experience.

Two of the three other girls with her that night "laugh and are not sure what they saw," she reports. "It's almost like their memories were erased or something."

She doesn't doubt what she saw, but she continues to contemplate the event's significance. "I'm not sure, but I think I've been chosen, perhaps for spiritual work of some kind," she guesses. "It has a lot to do with love, nature and God. I'm a Bible-believing Christian who was raised in a "holy roller" church, and I believe the Bible and science go together."

She describes herself as "a very, very loving individual, very, very forgiving, very much into nature and I love everything God has created."

She's been a bow hunter, but has now had second thoughts about taking the life of an animal. "Life is more precious to me," she says.

I ask if she harbors any latent fear from the experience.

"I have no fear of my destiny," she replies.

1976

Back in the harsh winter of 1976, 26-year-old April Crowe sure wasn't thinking about UFOs. If anyone had asked her for her thoughts about the subject, she would have told them that she was a skeptic.

She and her husband were living in an old ridge-top house that had no electricity, running water or phone. Caring for their two-year-old baby and carrying in water and fire wood was the order of the day. Every day.

One evening, about 10 p.m., April was standing at the kitchen window looking out into the night.

"Suddenly, I saw a bright light hanging over Cold Knob, a hill located about a quarter-mile away, and I thought it must be a helicopter. All the sudden, it moved to the left a quarter- to a half-mile, then stopped for about ten seconds. Then it shot straight up and disappeared.

"I wasn't afraid," she says now, "but I thought whatever that was, it was pretty weird."

Over the years since that time, April has spoken with friends who have told her they have seen space ships, sometimes with occupants in them, three- to four-foot tall beings who had big eyes, back in the hills and mountains around Trout, WV, where she and her husband live now.

1976

"I never did believe in stuff like this," the gruff voice says to me when I answer the phone on July 25, 1994, "but I'd be willing to take a lie detector test."

I assure Willis "Willie" Spencer that such is not necessary, and his voice returns to a grandfatherly-like, mid-range baritone.

Willie, who now lives in Mt. Storm, worked as a night (6 p.m. - 6 a.m.) security guard for the Crown Creek Coal Company in 1976 at the company's Beans Mill mine in Upshur County.

One night, some boys from homes in the area came over to Willie's guard shack with an incredible story. A woman, it seemed, had called police to rescue her from a "gray, hairy" monster which she had spotted on her porch. A short time later, according to the boys, police chased something into the nearby woods after wounding it with a gun shot.

"From the sound of it, I thought maybe it was an ape that had escaped from a zoo or something," Willie says. (Note: The French Creek Game Farm, a state-administered animal preserve, is a short distance away.)

Two days later, on his way home from work, Willie says he glimpsed something hiding behind a tree. "It had a hump on its back," just as the woman had apparently described it, he adds.

Two weeks later, while at work, Willie sat in his solitary, four-by six-foot guard shack in a quiet hollow listening to the radio and drinking a cup of coffee. "Now, I am not the kind of fellow to get scared," he tells me, "but all the sudden, I hear a sound like two pieces of metal slapping' together. It came from up in the hollow. And it startled me."

What he saw next has astounded him ever since.

"At first I thought it was a helicopter," he says. "Wellsir, I looked up and a big sort of headlight popped up, and then as it cleared the trees, my mouth flew open—

"It reminded me of a spinning top. It was about 40 to 50 feet in diameter, and was on maybe a 60-degree angle.

"A white beam of light come down, and another section of it turned orange. It wasn't spinning then.

"It had rectangular windows on it, top and bottom, and they were different colors, red, green, orange, purple. And they'd like go dim, then go real bright again.

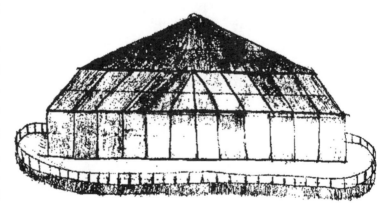

Willis "Willie" Spencer's hand-drawn likeness of the object he spotted while on guard duty at a Braxton County coal mine.

And each time they did that, it made a sound, like, '*va-room! va-room!*'

"The main part of it was gray, about the color of an elephant. And it had a deck around it, like a grate, with a railing on it that was maybe five feet high."

He watched it for approximately three minutes, and "in my mind, I thought either someone's inside it or it's remote control. I had a heck of a feeling. Even now when I think about it and how pretty it was, I get a happy feeling."

Eventually, the craft lifted up over the hill and was gone.

"There's never a week goes by without my thinking about it," Willie, 62, says. "I saw something that nobody else has seen before. I'm an honest and plain man," he adds, "and I treat people like I want to be treated."

The Beans Mill "monster" was never seen or heard from again.

Could its comrades have stopped by one night to pick it up, over there in that quiet, cleared area where there was nothing but a little guard shack?

The "bottom" of the craft, drawn by Mt. Storm resident, Willis "Willie" Spencer.

Interestingly, Willie Spencer's story bears a striking resemblance to the famous 1959 New Guinea sighting by the Reverend William Booth Gill (an Anglican priest) and others, who saw a large craft surrounded by a catwalk with a railing. In this case, individuals would walk out onto the catwalk and wave at the priest and other onlookers. (A full account of the story may be found in many books, including Keith Thompson's *Angels and Aliens: UFOs and the Mythic Imagination*, see bibliography.)

Chapter Eleven

Communion
In Sago

With the previous story having occurred in Upshur County, it is only right that I add the following accounts of other Upshur County sightings and experiences here.

On July 14, 1994, I receive a call from the most nervous person yet in this research.

Sandra Holmes begins by timidly interrogating me, like most callers who aren't quite sure of my motives. (Trust me, my motives are as pure as any researcher's, and as focused as any mortgagee's!)

Finally, she begins to open up.

She tells me of her July 3, 1994 sighting. (You'll find that in Chapter 13, beginning on Page 154.)

And then she gets down to business.

A few weeks later, I meet with Sandra, her ex-husband, Steve, and two other women in a wonderful, but noisy, Buckhannon restaurant— C.J. Maggie's—in the downtown area.

Cathy Collins, 47, is Director of Upshur County Emergency Services and 911. She lives in Buckhannon and has two UFO sightings of her own, dating back into the '60's.

I ask her to tell me what she knows about Sandra Holmes.

"We share an interest in UFOs and the supernatural. At one point, she called me and we talked about an incident she reportedly had had. Whether it affected herself, her husband and her children. Went into a lot of detail about it. She wanted me to confirm whether she was mentally off a little bit. She thought it may be something more related to the supernatural, psychic type situation. Not until Streiber's book *Communion* came out did I realize that what she had said was more like the experiences in the book.

I told her, and she said I was the one that was nuts, she wasn't going to touch that book with a 10-foot pole. Approximately five years later, I got her to read that book, promising her I would be at the other end of the telephone at the end of each chapter. She did read it. She called me. She couldn't believe what she had read that was so similar to what she had told me, before the book had been published."

"What prompted you to buy Strieber's book?" I ask.

"It dealt with aliens, I believe there are other forms of life out there. It appears to me that I have an affinity to the Pleiades. I can't tell you that I was there but I feel that's part of me. Every time I look into the sky, I automatically look for the Pleiades. If I can't see them I can hardly wait for them to come back up. I don't know why."

Here is Sandra's story. (Interview excerpts have been edited for clarity.)

Sandra Dean Holmes, 46, lives about seven miles outside of Buckhannon in a place called Sago.

I start by asking her about her interest in the supernatural.

Sandy: I just seemed to have incidents happen to me. I remember when I was a child... my aunt had died. I thought she had come to visit me one evening. I was in bed asleep. She had on a long filmy white dress. You could see through her. I wasn't absolutely convinced it was my aunt, but she was recently deceased and I just assumed it was. She walked around my bed, put her hand on my forehead. Her hand was cool. I kept thinking, "I hope this is my own hand on my forehead," but I realized my hands were down by my side. There was a third hand in there somewhere.

My father got up the next morning. He said, "What were you doing up playing cards all night?" I said I wasn't up out of bed at all last night. And he responded, "I heard you out there at the kitchen table shuffling cards all night long. Every time I got up to tell you to quit it and go to bed, you sneaked off on me."

Well, we didn't reconcile that one. He thought I did and I knew I didn't.

Little things like that got me interested.

Bob: Tell me about the night you saw a light in your bedroom back in the '70's.

Sandy: I remember lying on my back, which was unusual because I don't usually lie on my back. I woke up, or I was awake, and this little light about the size of a ping pong ball, came in through the window. It floated up above the bed and it just stopped. It was looking at us. Then it continued through this slow undulating fashion. It floated down below the transom, it didn't go through the wall. It was high enough to go through the wall, but instead it floated down through the door. Down the hallway into

> So, trying to be an amateur ghost buster, I was actually trying to will her in that night.

my sons' bedroom. When it got into their room, it exploded with a loud crack, and it was like a flash bulb had gone off in the room. A real bright light and a loud crack. And then suddenly, my children started screaming— they were screaming.

I said to (husband) Steve, "Go get them." I couldn't move. He said, "I can't move." I said, "I can't either." He did eventually get up and go down the hall into their bedroom. He came back, and said everything was all right. They laid right back down and went to sleep. I don't know if I was scared to death or what, I don't know why I couldn't move. I kind of pulled myself away from the force that was...and rolled over and went to sleep, like nothing had happened.

B: Do you think it's unusual that you didn't talk about it?

Sandy: Oh, yes. I have no idea why we didn't talk about it. We talked about everything else. But, I never met my grandmother and I always heard she was such a wonderful person, I really wanted to meet her. So, trying to be an amateur ghost buster, I was actually trying to will her in that night.

B: Before this experience?

Sandy: Yes. I wanted to tell her...I was concentrating very hard. I knew her house and was trying to get her to come and visit me. Concentrating earlier that evening in bed. Concentrated maybe 15 or 20 minutes. It's hard to say.

B: And you were well acquainted with occult literature?

Sandy: Maybe, barely. I think that's when I got more into it, around 1972 or '73.

B: Did you have the feeling, when the light was in the room, of anything spiritual?

Sandy: I remember saying to Steve, "Well, we're both on our backs. Do you see that?" He said yes. I just thought it was my grandmother. Then I scared myself, I thought, "If I'm that darn good, I'm going to give this up."

B: Anything I've missed with this incident.

Sandy: It didn't last more than three or four minutes.

B: If you thought that was your grandmother, why did you call me? Because you knew I was writing a UFO book?

Sandy: Whitley Streiber's book.

B: Do you have any memories like appeared in *Communion*?

Sandy: Yes, my kids screaming. It was like a flash bulb. The white blinding light absolutely filled their room and there was a noise associated with it. A loud crack. You couldn't make this sound with your hands. I associated it with electrical. Like a direct hit, a thunder storm.

Steven Allen Holmes, 49, is Sandra's ex-husband. He holds a degree in psychology, and is a pilot. He used to have as many as 100 people working for him in a natural gas and coal lease business, but the "market went to hell in '83 and '84," so he drastically scaled back the business and now deals in real estate.

> I was fascinated, petrified and immobile— all at the same time.

I ask for his version of what happened that night in the early 1970's.

Steve: I remember lying on my back, which is unusual. A light came through my window, just to my left. I have a cathedral ceiling, the light got up in that ceiling and bounced around. This didn't act like car lights when people get stuck in the road down there. It just bounced around, shot down and thru the bedroom into the hallway to our children's bedroom. I could hear the kids making noise like they were scared. I remember not being able to move. I couldn't get up. I couldn't will myself to get out of bed and go in. I just couldn't move. Then...it just disappeared. It wasn't very long, I can't put any time frame on it. There it was, I was fascinated, petrified and immobile— all at the same time.

Bob: How old were you then?

Steve: I was 26 or 27, 28 maybe. About 1972 -'73.

B: Did have any unusual thoughts during that episode?

Steve: Not anything specific. It just felt like it wasn't real. It didn't belong and it was very, it was eerie. I wasn't scared. It was different.

B: Did it try to communicate with you?

Steve: No, I felt like there had to be something directing it because it was unnatural movement. I remember hearing thoughts, but not sound. "We have to go to the kids." I remember my own thoughts, "I have to get

I didn't want to think it was anything other than a ball of light that bounced in the window, down the hall and bounced out.

up and go to the kids." Then background noise, like noise was all over the place but nothing I could identify. I could hear the kids, like they were scared. Two boys, Bryan, 4, Steve, 22 months. I don't remember the time of year. We didn't talk about it at the time. We didn't speak at all. It was later we decided it was her grandmother.

B: Do you think that's unusual?

Steve: Yeah, I didn't want to talk about. I don't know why. I think, looking back on it now, I didn't want to admit I couldn't move. I couldn't control myself. It's the same reason why I don't drink— I don't want to be out of control.

B: What did you do immediately after the light disappeared?

Steve: I think I stared at the ceiling for an hour or so and then I went to sleep. Can't remember anything else. I recall Sandy getting up later and going down to check on the kids, but I'm not sure of that, even. I don't think that even happened. I really can't remember. I know I didn't get up and check on them. I couldn't move.

B: Do you think that's unusual, that you didn't check on the kids?

Steve: Yeah, that's unusual. It was real unusual, but at that point I knew everything was okay. I knew they were fine. I knew I was okay, so I didn't want to get up and go check.

B: Did you attribute any spiritual significance to this?

Steve: It was spiritual in that we thought it was her grandmother. But that didn't make any sense. It was different.

B: Why did you think it was her grandmother?

Steve: Because we could explain that.

It could have been ball lightening, and so forth. There was no other explanation. But it didn't make sense, so I rejected it. But I didn't try to figure out what it was. I didn't believe it was anything other than strange. I didn't want to put a name to it. I didn't want to think it was anything other than a ball of light that bounced in the window, down the hall and bounced out.

B: Sandy, you've mentioned other experiences...

Sandy: I dreamed one night, can't imagine what else it would be, I was with another female. I knew her at the time but I don't know who she was now. We were in a very large building, very tall, large building. Lots of windows that went out into the front of this building. Maybe a cathedral type entrance. We were supposed to follow a yellow line on the floor. Wherever we were trying to go, we were instructed to follow the yellow line.

B: Instructed by whom?

> I woke up, went downstairs and I made a pot of coffee and read the Bible all night long.

Sandy: I don't know. I just knew I had to follow the yellow line to get to where I wanted to go. But, there was someone chasing us. It was a person, but, I got the impression this person was a zombie. Very tall and thin and gray, gray hair. The whole person was gray. His skin and clothes were the same color. No matter how fast we walked or ran, he was right behind us, but he wasn't running. He was just following us, and walking as fast as we were running and he was a zombie and he shouldn't be able to go that fast. Well, here we are following this yellow line, the line gets to the wall and it stops. And it goes up the wall and back across the ceiling. We didn't follow that yellow line anymore. I woke up, went downstairs and I made a pot of coffee and read the Bible all night long. I felt like it was the thing to do.

B: Tell me about this gray person.

Sandy: Very, very tall. He was gray. I don't remember his eyes. I remember he had facial features, just like an ordinary person.

B: Why did you think he was a zombie?

Sandy: I don't know.

B: What year was that?

Sandy: In the late 80's, maybe 1990. I also had a horrible nightmare about my son Bryan.

I was driving on the road between Reedsville and Kingwood (Preston County), on Rt. 7. There was a refrigerator truck in front of me, you could see the coils on the back of the truck just like the coils on the back of a refrigerator. Bryan and this darling little blonde, like maybe "Margaret" from the *Dennis the Menace* cartoon, in a little yellow dress, were both stuck behind this refrigeration coil, between the truck and the coil. And they couldn't get out. I was trying to catch the truck to stop it so I could get my kid out of there. Something kept telling me in my dream that those coils were going to get real hot here real soon and I had to get them out of there. I woke up terrified. That was another night I went downstairs and read the Bible. I don't sleep in my bedroom, I sleep on my couch every night.

B: Why?

Sandy: I don't have nightmares when I sleep on the couch. I sleep with the TV on all night long, the channel goes off at 2 a.m. but it still goes '*psssssss.*'

B: What are you concerned about that makes you do that?

Sandy: I have no idea. I live alone, out in the country. I'm not afraid.

B: Have you seen any other UFOs?

Sandy: I did see a UFO around Sago. Or something that didn't crash into the mountain that should have.

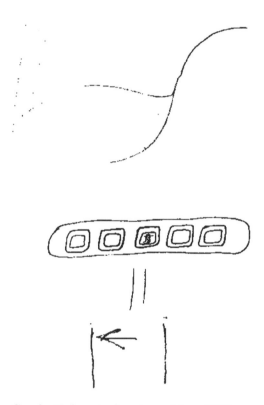

It was early in the morning, it was light enough to see. In the winter time. I got my coffee and I was standing at the kitchen sink looking down the valley. There comes this craft and went '*whoosh*'...like that, across my line of sight. It was too close...it was not a plane or a helicopter. From the side it looked like this (see drawing).

It was gray, dull gray-type of metal. Almost looked like an old car that had gray primer on it. I can't remember the shape of the windows, if they were round or square. The windows looked like they had depth to them, like they were all the way down the craft. No sparks, no lights, nothing on top or bottom. The windows went all the way down the side with spaces in between them. It was almost like looking at an airplane, side view without the wings. I could almost swear, like there were people in these windows looking out. They looked like, maybe not in every window, just a...kind of a form. Maybe even a little bowler on their head. Just one little form. But

Sandy Holmes's drawing of her UFO sighting. The object flew quickly past her kitchen window (in the drawing, from right to left as indicated by the arrow), and appeared to have an occupant or occupants looking out a window back at her. The little forms or form seemed to be wearing a hat, like a "bowler." The lines in the upper part of the drawing represent hills, which continue on around to the side, and into which Sandy thinks the craft disappeared.

I got the impression that thing was looking at me.

It had to be a flying saucer to be flying that low and not crash into the hill. I remember sitting down at the table, drinking my coffee. Thinking, I'm not going to tell anybody about this. But I did 'cause that morning on the news they said several people in Emoryville called to report a UFO. I said, "Hey, there was one in Sago, too."

B: Recall now, the instant you made eye contact, when you thought something was looking at you.

Sandy: It's almost like I can see a hand, or an arm, or a stick or something attached to this thing. It was ...I kind of remember something looking out at me through the window.

Sandra Holmes talks about her experiences. Photo by Bob Teets.

B: Where's the hill?

Sandy: (Draws) Here's the top of the hill, trees on it, hay shed. This thing flew between this hill and me. It went into the side of the hill.

B: Did you see it go into the hill?

Sandy: No. It disappeared behind these trees. It would have had to have crashed into the hill. It was so low. I only saw it for two seconds, maybe three. No glow or lights like an explosion. It couldn't have risen fast enough to avoid the hill. It's right behind my house, extends around a ridge.

B: You're saying the craft went into the hill?

Sandy: I didn't see it go into the hill. I'm saying it had to go into the hill. I didn't hear it crash.

The old man who lives up on the hill, he confessed to his son, he had seen something that reminded him of a shotgun shell. There was a cloud hanging over his house. He said this shotgun shell-shaped thing came tumbling down out of the clouds. He never told anybody, years ago. This was in '85.

B: Did you ever see that saucer again?

Sandy: No.

B: Imagine for a second that this craft, this shape, this thing was your soul. And your soul was trying to give you a message. What message did

116

this story tell you?

Sandy: That these things do exist. And there goes one. 'I'll be back, I shall return...'

I don't know if you took any notice of my son Bryan, but he has this huge scar on his arm. It's a very ugly, huge scar. He fell through a trailer window, playing around an old abandoned trailer on a gob pile. He slipped and his arm went through this window. Severely cut him and he almost bled to death before we got him to the hospital. He had to walk quite a ways to get help and it was only a miracle that there were people at a house out there.

Later, after they stitched him up at the hospital, I was praying, on my hands and knees beside his bed. All of a sudden, I opened my eyes and there was this little familiar white ping pong ball of light bouncing up and down right over his head board. I thought, well, that must be his guardian angel and I was thanking that guardian angel.

B: The same ping pong ball that—

Sandy: —yes.

B: That's like part of the difference in how people perceive this UFO phenomena. Do you feel special?

Sandy: Yes. Just the fact that I've seen these things. Kills me to have to leave Sago. I don't like to shop. I like to go into the woods. I go to the river for quiet time. I've had an affinity for Sago all my life.

I again turn my attention to Steve.

Bob: Describe some of your other precognitive experiences.

Steve: I was asleep and woke up, straight out of bed. Sat up straight in bed, which again, is unusual because, normally, I don't sleep on my back. I had seen, there was a blinding flash of light, people—fire, people in the water, and that's all. The next day it was announced in the news that a ferry boat in Sweden had exploded and 140-some people (had been killed).

I had seen a person two days before they died, now I can't remember who the person was. I saw the death mask and knew they were going to die. That's happened to me before.

I have actually pulled off the road to get out of the way of a vehicle that was going to be on my side without being able to see that vehicle coming. Pull off the road and stop and wait for it to come. And it did.

I think that's a coincidence, but it happens a lot.

B: Can you consciously initiate this state of awareness?

Steve: No, 'cause I think I try not to have it happen. I don't want it. It's less frequent now then it was. The last two or three years, I've not experienced much. I try not to...

B: Were you aware of either of your parents having this ability?

Steve: My mother had....she never spoke about it much either, but talked about being able to "know" that something was going to happen.

I try to forget about this. I've never read any of those books those guys were talking about. I don't want to read those books.

B: How do you explain any of these experiences you've had, either the precognitive experiences or the light in your room, from a psychological aspect?

Steve Holmes discusses his ESP abilities, which he says he tries to ignore. Photo by Bob Teets.

Steve: As if I were talking about somebody else's?

B: Yes.

Steve: The denial part, the thing I don't want to deal with, is outside of what I know is normal. I would suggest that is in the realm of normal for most people and they don't know it. The ability of ESP, and so forth rests in most people, but either they choose to ignore it or they are scared by it. I fall in that category. I choose to ignore it because I can't control it. I need to be in control.

Bob: Any other instances where you remember encountering UFOs or anything strange?

Steve: I'm a pilot since '73. We were flying back from Ft. Lauderdale, Florida, and the weather was bad west of Roanoke (Virginia). I saw this light on my left. It caught my attention and it was a green ball. It looked like it might have been four or five miles away from us on the left wing.

My company pilot, who was co-piloting with me, said he saw it, too. About that time the radio came alive and we were on an Eastern Airlines path, and all the airline pilots were talking about seeing this light. They weren't saying it was a UFO, they were only saying it was a green light.

We watched if for about five minutes before it disappeared. It was on a straight course. We were traveling about 200 m.p.h., at 180 or so knots. It came from my left about head high and descended at an angle less than 45 degrees and it just went into the ground and disappeared. At least it looked like it disappeared. I couldn't see where it went in. I didn't see smoke or a flash, it was just gone. I never read anything about it afterwards.

B: What did you guys think it was?

Steve: We did talk about it on the ground. Nobody would say it was anything other than a light. At that time, if a pilot did report a UFO, the pilot went through quite a lengthy debriefing. I don't know if that's still true.

After speaking with Cathy Collins and the Holmes', I turn my attention to Suzanne Ocheltree, 31, who is Steve Holmes's secretary. I thought she had joined us for lunch and to observe the others while they told their stories.

We talk for only a minute, though, when I find that she, too, has a story.

Suzanne: In July of '89, I was a manager for McDonald's. We had just closed the store for the day. The four people that closed with me, sometimes we would go out camping together, so we were always looking for places to go.

So, this night one of the guys said, "Let's go out on the Red Rock Road," which is west of Buckhannon.

It was 1 a.m., so as we started up the road, I told them, there were five of us, I said, "I don't want to go. Something is going to happen and I do not want to go." I was very adamant and I had this terrible feeling of fear and dread.

We pulled off the road and got out. The person who had suggested we come here said, "You know, everybody says that house up there on the hill is haunted." He had parked the car so you could see up across the hill. It's an old abandoned farm house, and I said, "I want to leave, now."

They said they would go down in this field and see about a place to camp, so they all got out of the car and asked if I were coming. I said, "I'm not staying in here by myself, but I'm telling you, I do not want to do this."

We walked up the road, down over a bank and across an old fence that had fallen down. One of the boys went on ahead of us.

But then I could hear him coming back. I heard him before I saw him. I was in front. He came running back to me and his face was just white and his eyes were huge. I thought he was just trying to scare me 'cause he came right up to me. I said, "Stop it right now or I'll beat the living daylights out of you!"

He started to talk, and I said, "What is wrong with you?" He said, "It's behind me! It's coming after me!" I said, "Stop it! I'm leaving right now."

At that time, I looked right past him and we all, I think, saw it at the same time. Nobody said anything. It was like an eternity that we stood there, but it was probably less than 15 seconds.

It was a dark form, about 6 feet or so tall, in the shape of a large man. But it had no features, and it was probably about three yards from us. It was standing right in the middle of the path.

It was a dark form, black on black. It had green eyes, big green eyes.

I think I said a few things I shouldn't have, but then I said, "Let's get the hell out of here!"

We all took off in a dead run. We had to go up over the bank, beside this field, to get back to the car.

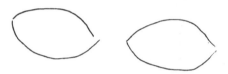

The haunting eyes that Suzanne Ocheltree said were staring at her from a "black on black" form which terrorized her camping friends in 1989.

We were all running, and I didn't realize it before but we were all trying to stay together. At one point I glanced over my shoulder to make sure we were all okay and it was still standing there. You could see the eyes and I knew it was like, following us.

We all nearly killed ourselves getting into the car and the person who was driving, trying to get the key into the ignition, I said, "Just get us out of here!"

None of us said a word the whole way back. The car was absolutely silent. We got back to the parking lot at McDonald's, and I said, "I need to know what you all saw. I cannot get out of this car until I know what you all saw."

We all saw exactly the same thing. It was not an animal, it was not a bear, I know that because my father works for the DNR, so I've been around a lot of animals. We really do not know what it was. But we all had fear, real fear. There was a feeling of evil.

After all this happened, I heard stories about teenagers being in the area....satanic rituals if you will. They said there were emblems painted on the walls of the old house. People said things did go on out there, but I heard this about a year after we had been there. The police had investigated it.

I don't know where it came from. I do believe in the supernatural. I do believe there is a God. I believe there is life in other places. But I don't know if it was an alien. It scares me to think about it.

While we sit at the table, Steve listens to Suzanne's story, then draws the figure below. "That's it," Suzanne says with a shivver.

Chapter Twelve

Mountain Fireworks: 1980's Style

1984

It was 1984—George Orwell's anticipated year of "Big Brother's" zenith.

To many, Orwell's prediction had come true. Privacy had become a thing of the past. Congress seemed hell-bent on tossing the Constitution out in favor of a more "efficient" concept based on "Reaganomics." Orwellian-like technology was said to be up and running as part of our futuristic StarWars space-based antimissile defense system, and yet, talks between the U.S. and the Soviet Union were bringing us closer to extinction. If that weren't enough, Arch Moore, Jr. was reelected to his third term as governor of West Virginia (which would lead him to a sort of Orwellian hell of his own— as an inmate at the Ashland, KY, Federal Correctional Institute following his 1990 guilty plea for extortion, obstruction of justice, mail fraud and tax law violations[1]).

But there was good news, too. Two West Virginians won Olympic Gold at the XXIII Olympiad in Los Angeles: Fairmont gymnast Mary Lou Retton, and Morgantown small-bore shootist, Ed Etzel[2].

Nonetheless, and according to a trusted friend, "Times were weird."

Weird was probably the word that three friends would have used one night in the summer of 1984 near the TNT area of Point Pleasant (the place where the "Mothman" was first seen in the 1960's—see Page 9 for a brief accounting of that case) when they saw "fireworks" coming across the Ohio River, straight for them.

---

1. Thanks to *Charleston Daily Mail* syndicated political columnist Richard Grimes and newspaper staffers for providing research on the list of charges to which Gov. Moore pled guilty.

2. Thanks, too, to Morgantown *Dominion Post* Sports Editor Mitch Vingle for providing Ed's name.

When the trio spotted what Jeff Rife describes as "the outline of a symmetrical object that was transparent in the middle with six lights around it," he took off running—

—towards it.

"Come get me! I wanna' go!" he recalls yelling as he ran.

Jeff, now 29, says it appeared close, and yet it was in sight and coming towards them a very long time, several minutes in fact.

His friend, Keith Pridemore (whom I contacted in a follow-up interview) agrees. "It sure seemed like a long time," he says.

And once the object reached their position, Jeff and Keith agree that it slowed down.

"It seemed real close," Keith states, "like it was no more than 50-100 yards away from us, coming in at an angle. Its lights, around a dozen, were shining straight down on us. I remember thinking, 'What's going to happen next?' I thought it may beam us up."

The next thing they knew, the object was speeding off in the same direction.

"It never made a turn," Jeff says.

The day after the incident, Jeff remembers seeing something on the news about a Russian satellite burning up in the atmosphere. "I didn't believe it," he adds firmly. His friend, Keith, agrees. "I don't see how it could have been a satellite," he says. "It was awful close the ground."

Interestingly, both men say they were thinking about the incident only the week before, even though they haven't seen each other for years.

(NOTE: I could not locate the third friend for an interview, and so far, I haven't been able to find an account of burning space debris entering earth's atmosphere during the summer of 1984.)

1984

About 20 miles south and only a few months after the triple sighting described in the preceding story, 50-year-old Franklin (not his real name) and a nephew were squirrel hunting in Cabell County.

Though it was still daylight, Franklin happened to look up toward the north/northwest and spot the moon, so while he called his nephew's attention to it, "*zip!*— up comes a UFO," he says.

His nephew was terrified. But Franklin wasn't.

"My mind went through every possibility except it being a UFO," he recalls. "My mind raced so fast to put it in perspective that I didn't have time to be afraid."

He trained his 10 X 50 binoculars on it.

Then another UFO came into view.

Instantly, he knew what was about to happen. "I had the distinct impression it was going to come over and land, so I tried to tell it telepathically that my nephew would die if it did," he says, adding that he is familiar with ESP because he and his mother use it all the time.

Apparently, it worked.

"It took off," he says.

Since that time, he has considered many possibilities in trying to explain the sighting. "UFOs have expanded our horizons," he says. "We're in the horse and buggy days of space travel compared to what they saw that day. The Bible talks about UFOs."

But Franklin admits that he is "still trying to find logic to the whole damn thing."

1982
Letter Excerpt

"It was October 18, 1982. The winds were turning cold beneath cyan-blue dusk as the last remnants of summer were vanquished. I remember the evening as vividly as if it had happened yesterday.

"A friend of the family had just brought a truckload of coal which we unloaded into the basement of our home. After we had finished...I remained outside for a time to cool off. It was nearly completely dark now, and the sky was absolutely clear. I turned my gaze westward, toward the ridge.

"The place where I lived was about two miles up in a hollow called Browning Fork. It was the widest part of the hollow and certainly the most scenic. The mountains around our home were like any other in the area, but the ridge was different, or at least it was to me. It was long and flat, except for a small 'hump' at the south edge. Though the sky was nearly completely dark, the sun sat behind the ridge, silhouetting it against the skyline.

"As I watched, I noticed a single starlike speck in the skyline just above the ridge, moving from North to South. It was not physically ON the ridge, because there was a noticeable gap between the object and the ridge. I thought nothing of it at first because I had seen many airplanes in the area look similar to that at night. But approximately three seconds after the light was visible, I noticed another light giving chase, maintaining a precise distance from the first one. The two lights proceeded across the ridge at a constant speed and maintained their precise separation.

"Abruptly, halfway across the ridge, both lights stopped. Now understand, they did not slow down then stop, they simply stopped dead in their tracks, as if they were a part of a machine. As soon as they stopped, a third light appeared as if spawned by the first light. It came away from the other two at the same speed as the first two were travelling, and stopped just as abruptly when all three lights had approximately the same distance between them.

"The three mysterious lights hung motionless for a few seconds, I'm not exactly sure how many. Then, as abruptly and mechanically as they had stopped, they started moving again. The first two proceeded back northward along the ridge and the singular "spawned" light proceeded southward at the same speed. The entire incident took no more than thirty seconds. Not a single sound could be heard at any time.

"What did I see? I have no idea. Being a licensed pilot, I know of no conventional aircraft that can move with that kind of precision and abruptness. But the incident was so awesome to me that I will never forget it, and I will never stop searching for the truth."

Sincerely,
John Nagle

1970 and 1986

Kathleen (not her real name) was 10 years old in 1970 when she and some friends were playing one summer day in the yard.

"I glanced up," she says, "and there it was, a fuzzy, black disc, just like pictures that typically depict UFOs. I always remembered it. All I really thought was, 'Wow!'"

Sixteen years later, in the spring of 1986, Kathleen was driving home from work as a store clerk.

On Rt. 73 outside of Bridgeport, about a half-mile from her home, "there was an airplane over there," she says. "I remember it was cylinder-shaped. When I slowed down for a closer look, that's all I remember. That plane was flying really low."

She had a dream later that night.

"I was in a place with a lot of rooms, and there were lots of body parts laying around. I came to the bathroom where everything was stainless steel. My new daughter was lying there with a leg cut off and blood spurting everywhere."

She awoke from the nightmare, and "my head was pointed toward the doorway. I thought I saw something about two or three feet tall running out. I experienced total terror."

After that, she had nightmares for six years, and says, "I changed a lot."

She quit going to church, "completely lost interest," she explains. And now, "I'm not interested in organized religion. But I hope there's a God."

Another change she noticed was a striking "fascination with English history, particularly the Tutor kings. I read every book I can find about them." She had never had such an interest before the second sighting.

"It's still upsetting to me," Kathleen, 33, says, and yet, "I am very fascinated with the idea of UFOs."

(Note: I had asked Kathleen if she would be interested in a hypnosis session. She responded positively, so we tentatively agreed that I would call within the next few weeks to arrange a session. About 10 days later, I called. Her phone number had been changed to an unlisted number. I'm still trying to find her.)

1980 and 1987

Christian Harper remembers sitting in his parent's van outside a Little Caesar's Pizza place somewhere in Michigan around 1980. He was seven years old at the time.

"I looked out, and there was a small object just hovering over the van," he says. "And that's all I remember."

Seven or eight years later, while living in the Country Road Mobile Home Park in Poca, Putnam County, he experienced a more memorable sighting.

"I was 14, and about 9:30 one night, I looked out the window of my room and I saw a UFO. About 150-200 yards away, it looked like an up-side-down ice cream cone with blue rings all around it. I watched it about 45-seconds, and then it landed on top of the hill. It was silent."

He called his father to come see, "but Dad wouldn't listen. I couldn't sleep the rest of the night."

There were approximately 40 mobile homes in the park, but no one else reported a sighting.

When word of Christian's sighting got out, he says the other kids in the park started calling him "Martian Boy."

He started keeping a camera in bed with him after that sighting, but he hasn't seen anything since.

Christian is attending Marshall University, where he hopes to become an R.N. He also takes care of his grandmother.

"I believe in other intelligences, and I'm intrigued by science, but I also believe in a Higher Power," he says.

Late '70's or 1980

Mr. and Mrs. George Opas of Fairmont saw a "big, white," saucer-shaped craft come from a long way off and land on a hill about ¼ mile from their house. They watched from their terrace while a "red ball" shot out of it and proceeded to fly toward Interstate 79. It would then return, and the craft would leave, becoming smaller and smaller as it receded over the horizon.

The interesting thing here is that this scene repeated itself every night—for a month, according to Mrs. Opas.

On another occasion, George was heading south on I-79 at dusk one evening and saw "something with a few lights and six windows" about 150 feet over top of his car. He pulled over to watch it, and he could then see that the object was saucer-shaped.

Another motorist pulled over to watch, and he and George chatted about it for a while, until the craft moved off to the south.

Returning home, George called the newspaper and was told that no other calls had come in about any UFO sightings.

1984

Letter Excerpt:

"A possible UFO—Flying Saucer hovered over Sleepy Creek Mountain to the Southeast of us for a few minutes, maybe longer...somewhere around 10 p.m., some 10 years ago. It came in slowly from the South, stopping short of the Sleepy Creek Mountain Fire Lookout Tower. This tower was removed a couple years ago.

"As close as I can remember, it had lights, but nothing

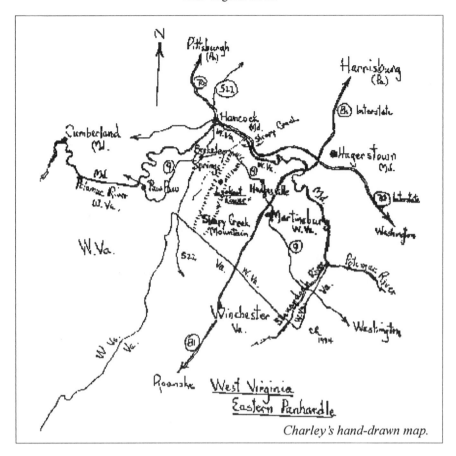

Charley's hand-drawn map.

spectacular...and it occasionally moved up and down and maybe sideways. Most of the time it was stationary. Helicopters move up and down, too, but helicopters make a lot of noise. There was no noise. Then, the one criteria I've always looked for, but had never seen—happened.

"Suddenly—very suddenly, that UFO took off, in a southerly direction back the way it had come—with incredible speed. It seemed to be following the ridge, though, in the darkness, it could have been rising or climbing rapidly.

"In short, from a standing position—and before I could collect my wits— it was out of sight. All in silence.

"Another possible sighting may have been the 'bread truck incident.'

"One morning, I stopped in at Mike's Food Store in Berkeley Springs for a fresh loaf of bread. Both Mike and the Food Store are no longer with us. But no bread. So I asked Mike, 'Where's the bread?' His reply had to do with the fact the bread truck never made it in this morning. Somebody had called to tell him, or Mike had called the Bread Company—more likely, it had been stopped on Rt. 9 just west of Hedgesville, by a UFO which hovered low over the road in front of the truck—scaring the daylights out of the driver. Believe it was before daylight. Anyway, he wasted no time in turning around and heading back 'for home.'

"Did you ever read *Brighter Than a Thousand Suns* by Robert Jungk (a reporter)? Page 87. Copyright 1956 and 1958, Harcourt, Brace and Co. Library of Congress card #58-8581. A footnote says:

"'The only exception to the lack of interest shown by authorities was constituted by the Air Ministry. The Air Force research workers were in a peculiar position. They produced interesting new types of aircraft such as the Delta (triangular) and *flying discs*. The first of these *flying saucers*, as they were later called...circular in shape, with a diameter of some 45-yards...were built by the specialists Schriever, Habermohl and Miethe. They were first airborne on February 14, 1945, over Prague and reached in three minutes a height of nearly eight miles. They had a flying speed of 1250 m.p.h. which was doubled in subsequent tests. It is believed that after the war Habermohl fell into the hands of the Russians. Miethe developed at a later date similar flying saucers at A.V. Roe and Company for the United States.'"

Charlie Rowland
Berkeley Springs, WV

(Note: I have not been able to find a copy of the book, but I am most thankful for Charlie's citation. There are many other sources of information about saucer development during and after World War II, including rumors about heavily fortified German research facilities, but I do not know of their veracity. The craft depicted on the front cover of this book is, according to one source, a drawing of the *"Ballenzo-Schriever-Miethe Disc,"* from the book, *Matrix*, by Valdamar Valerian, copyright 1988, with permission. I chose the illustration for many obvious reasons.)

1985

In 1985, North American Fastener Corporation line supervisor Gary Lafferty, 38, was driving along East Main Street in Clarksburg on his way home from work one summer night when a blinking star caught his attention.

Suddenly, the star shot down to the left in a straight line perhaps a

Gary Lafferty's drawing of his sighting.

hundred miles, then stopped and blinked. Then it shot over to the right an equal distance, paused, blinked, then it zoomed up to the left and back to its original position, where it blinked again.

Gary, an admitted UFO skeptic, pulled his truck over on to the berm and watched.

Again and again for the next five minutes the light repeated the pattern, "a perfect triangle," Gary says. "I felt like it didn't want me to leave, like it was pulling me out of my truck."

So, he exited the vehicle and continued watching. "I couldn't pull myself away."

A short while later, the light disappeared "in the wink of an eye."

Gary isn't sure, but he thinks the object may have had a purpose. "It seemed as if it were taking pictures of a whole continent, it was so far up," he says.

1983

William Tracy Miller was walking up his driveway on Kentuck Hill, Jackson County, one day in 1983 when he glanced over to the horizon. There, flipping end to end, were what appeared to be three football-shaped objects, equally spaced, rolling along. They stopped when he saw them, then continued on their journey.

He sort of "sluffed it off." That is, until sometime later he was talking with an 80-year-old neighbor woman about UFOs. He hadn't yet told her about his sighting, when she began telling him about seeing three footballs moving along the horizon 20 years previously.

That started him wondering.

Then, six years later (1989), and living at a different location, he was out in his yard one evening practicing martial arts, and glanced up.

"It was huge and pyramid-shaped," he says. "It had steady burning lights on it, and domes on the top and bottom that looked like the bomber turrets you see on old airplanes. The windows in the turrets had panes in them.

"I ran inside," he confesses, "this one tripped me out!"

In early September, he says, he was watching the "Crusaders" television program and was "amazed when they showed three football-shaped UFOs—just like the ones I saw!"

Received the Following Reports at the Last Minute of our Deadline:

1980

Judith Jones from Spencer (Clay County), looked out her bathroom

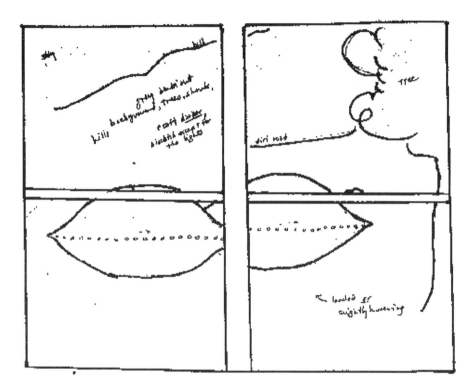

window (see drawing below) late one evening and, to her surprise, clearly saw two identical, large crafts either resting on the ground or hovering slightly above it no more than 50 feet away. Six lights flashed in a strobing pattern from left to right around the perimeter of both craft's 18 to 25-foot diameter. A few seconds later, the objects sped off, one straight up, and the other, sideways.

Judith went to bed, she says.

Date Unknown

Helen Risher of Morgantown was traveling with her sister one summer day in nearby Pennsylvania, when suddenly they spotted a round, disc-shaped object hovering nearby. "It dipped its edge like in a greeting," she says, and then it turned and disappeared over a hill. "With God as my judge, I saw it very plainly," she says. "It's gospel."

1965

Tom R. (not his real name) tells the following story:

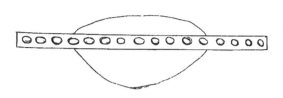

"We were back in Valley Head, WV (Randolph County) visiting in the summertime. It was 9:30 p.m. and a group of us kids were playing hide and seek, I was 11 years old at the time. I ran around the side of the hill to find a place to hide. I looked up the hollow and there it was! A round, disc-shaped object (see his drawing, above) hovering about 50' above the trees. It had red flashing lights running around it and appeared to be about 15' to 20' across. I watched it for 30 seconds or less. It shot across the sky—crossed town in a couple of seconds—toward Webster Springs, Point Mountain. I ran back and told the other kids what I had seen, no one else saw it. The way it was situated in the hollow, it would have been hard for anyone else to see.

"It had an egg shaped dome on top of the flat part.

"I know what I saw, I would go to my grave knowing what I saw. It totally surprised me. I ran around the side of the hill, saw it, and thought, 'What is that?' It was right in my face, about 150 to 200 yards away from me. I froze when I first saw it, it really scared me. I know I saw a UFO—no question whatsoever.

"There is no doubt in my mind what I saw. It shocked me, it scared me, and I was impressed. I was awestruck. It's as fresh to me today as when I saw it."

He had one other sighting.

"One summer evening in 1973 or '74 about 1:00 a.m. I was driving back from Deep Creek Lake (Garrett County, MD). It was at Shorty's Tavern on Rt. 219 in Pleasant Valley, it's real open and flat through there.

"I was driving along, looked up and to the left. It was a clear night, lots of stars and I saw this red ball of light. It really caught my attention because it was bigger than normal plane lights, about the size of a softball, and it was hovering up in the sky.

"I pulled off to see what it was. It broke into three lights and each light took off in a different direction and disappeared. I watched it for about 45 seconds before it blew apart and disappeared. I could see a light trail, like a blur as they disappeared. I thought, 'What the heck is it? I know it's not normal.'"

Chapter Thirteen

90's Sightings Keep Skies Bright

During the summer while I traveled around the state, it surprised me to hear so many people think there had been no recent UFO sightings in West Virginia.

In fact, and if my foray into the state's sightings is any indicator, it seems as if the number is increasing—*rapidly*.

Here's a sampling.

1993

Beckley (Raleigh County) interior decorator and seamstress Linda Linkus has "seen so many weird things over the years" that she's beginning to wonder if something is "keeping tabs on me."

Her most recent sighting occurred last December, just off of one of the busiest exits from I-64 in the city, the Harper Road exit. Amidst dozens of fast food restaurants, motels, hotels and gas stations, Linda looked up to see a "real bright light, so bright it hurt your eyes," hovering directly above the Go-Mart convenience store. She pulled over and watched it for a long time before it finally moved slowly off.

She tells a most intriguing story of being one of hundreds of people stranded on an interstate highway outside of Hagerstown, Maryland

Linda Linkus at the Go-Mart store.

one evening in 1966 when a giant, orange craft hovered over a restaurant while Army National Guard units in tanks held the craft at bay.

On another occasion, this time at a popular camping spot on the banks of the New River, close to Shanklin's Ferry (Summers County), she saw a mysterious, bright blue light shining from the other side of an embankment. When she investigated, she discovered that the "beautiful" light was flashing from beneath the water. She hopes there are others who have seen it, because "being the first to see these things" is upsetting to her.

Her grandmother, she says, believes that such things are a sign of the devil.

"It bothers me after I see these things," she says. "My personal opinion is, I'd rather not see them. That bugs me."

1960's - June, 1994

Nancy Workman has had a slew of sightings. The 68-year-old Huntington resident is not afraid of them, either.

"When I see one, I think, 'If you are alive, God created you, so I'm not afraid,'" she states.

When she was in her 20's, she recalls her doctor in San Francisco (where she lived at the time) telling her that she had called him one day to come and rescue her from a certain location because she had not known how she had ended up there. She had no conscious memories of calling him, nor of being lost somewhere.

In the 1960's, she was visiting some relatives and, standing on the porch one day, they watched some sort of object "hanging over top of the hill. It was long with lights on it."

She had another unusual experience on February 28, 1976.

"My mother had passed away, so I was at the old home place at Elk Creek for her funeral. Now, my mother didn't want any drinking at her funeral because she was a very Christian woman, and my father had been a Baptist preacher," so Nancy had worked to assure that would be the case.

After the funeral, "I walked out into the yard alone, and it seems like I was surrounded by a golden glow of some kind. I didn't want to leave it. I looked up in the heavens and I told my mother that everything went fine at her funeral, no drinkin' or anything like that." The light then somehow answered her message with a feeling of warmth and love which she did not want to relinquish. Nonetheless, it faded slowly away.

"We called death 'crossing the crystal waters' back in those days, when 'viewings' of the deceased would occur at the family's home instead of a funeral home" she says, "and we used to cover mirrors in the house when someone died. We also put a saucer of salt on the person in the casket, and pennies on their eyes." She is unsure why people did such things, but she accepted the tradition.

Nancy is psychic, as well.

She remembers one time seeing "... my son on a horse crossing the crystal waters, the wind blowing his hair," a very short time before she was notified that the son had died in a fire in 1978.

Often, she "hears church choir music and bells" at the moment someone in the family dies. "Before Dad died, I heard his voice in the choir," she recalls. "I don't hear it with the young ones in the family who die."

More recent sightings occurred on April 23 and 30, May 28, and June 4, 1994.

"My husband called my attention to the (April 23) object. There was a bright light in the sky near Huntington shooting things out of it. I thought it was a star, but it was cloudy and there were no stars out."

On the subsequent sightings, there would be more than one object, and one would "shoot something out of it that would look like a big, long streak of light that went out for miles, but then it would come back."

1964 and 1994

It was the night before Joe Pickens' turn as lookout aboard a 125-man Coast Guard ship on routine duty 625 miles east of Bermuda. The ship had just been outfitted with sophisticated new radar.

On this night in 1964, the lookout whose duty it was to scan the sea for anything and everything, called down to the wheelhouse through the nearby voicetube that he had spotted a "light on the horizon." The radar officer below reported a clear screen, no bogies.

Sometime later, the lookout once again called down that it was ship. Moments passed and he repeated his statement, adding that it was getting closer.

Still, radar wasn't tracking anything.

A short time later, officers in the wheelhouse could hear the lookout screaming, "Help! They're coming after me!"

A search for the lookout eventually located him, clinging to a 24" searchlight. He was rescued, taken to sick bay, then eventually shipped off to a hospital.

"We all thought the guy had gone crazy or was just trying to get out of watch duty," Joe recalls.

But the next night was Joe's turn as lookout.

"I told my buddies I was going to take a gun with me," he laughs.

Later that night, however, he wasn't laughing.

"I was worried. I saw a light like the other man had seen, off the starboard bow. I reported it, and the guys in the wheel-house started kidding me. But it got closer and closer. It

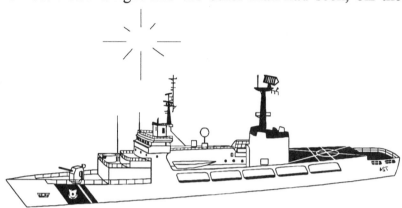

sort of looked like a star on the horizon. There was nothing on radar.

"The next thing I knew, it started getting real close, and it came up to within 300-400 yards of the ship!"

By that time, many men were watching, some taking pictures.

"It set there for about five minutes. I could see it move, but I couldn't tell its shape or size. At one point a 100-foot long illuminated tube like a flexible fluorescent light or a rubber hose lit up and came down out of this, thing. And then, all at once, it took off quickly at two or three times its approach speed.

"Later, the CIC (Combat Information Center) guys said they tracked it at 1,800 m.p.h. as it went out. There was nothing in 1964 that could go that fast," he says, adding he heard later that the ship's captain had radioed the sighting to a base on Bermuda, and three jets had been scrambled.

Joe's second sighting occurred on land and over his house in Given (Jackson County) in March or April of 1994.

Because he is a ham radio operator, Joe often goes outside at night to peer at the horizon in order to see spacecraft which may be coming up over the horizon. He often communicates with the Muir Space Station and other manned vehicles in earth orbit.

This evening, however, as he peered into the sky, hundreds of stars appeared to be blacked out in a certain area of the sky. As he stood watching it, he could make out the shape of a huge, black triangle silently drifting across the sky. It was hard to estimate distance with only the stars as a backdrop, but Joe says, "it was a good 100 feet, front to back."

He could see stars disappearing, then reappearing as the object moved overhead.

November, 1991 (Letter Excerpt):

"At that time (November, 1991), I was a coal miner working the 4 p.m.-midnight shift. I left the mine at 12:30 a.m. to go to Highland County, Virginia, deer hunting. I was on Rt. 460 going north about 20 miles from Bluefield, W. Va. The night was clear with a few scattered clouds and a full moon. Visibility was excellent.

"I noticed an object in the sky moving east to west. It appeared suddenly as out of nowhere. It was travelling at a slow rate of speed and had no night lights. After a few seconds, it turned onto its side and then I saw it was aluminum-colored

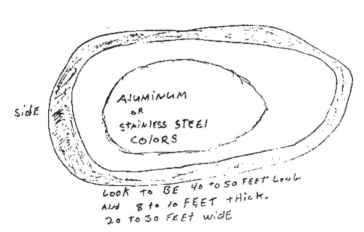

and oval-shaped (see drawing above). I rolled my truck window down and could not hear any sound.

"There was one puffy cloud low in the sky which the object moved into. I could see three sides of the cloud and the object did not move out of the cloud as I could see.

"I watched the cloud for about 15 minutes. I was driving toward it and had no difficulty observing it and the highway, too. I was travelling about 35 m.p.h.

"I finally pulled onto the shoulder of the highway and observed the cloud for another 10 minutes. As I did not see the object again, I continued on to my destination.

"My truck was the only vehicle on the road that night.

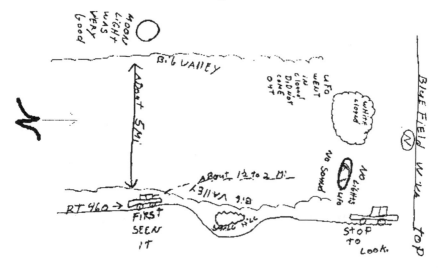

"Now some facts about myself: I am a 54-year-old family man and have worked hard all my life. I am an ex-navy man, don't drink alcohol, and have never been in trouble with the law. I am truthful, levelheaded, with common sense. I am not given to flights of fantasy.

"I hope this info is of some help to you."

Sincerely,
John O'Brien
Grundy, VA

1990

James Unroe could see that a fierce storm was brewing this day when he worked at the International Nickel Company in Huntington, so he thought he had better go outside to take care of a chore before it hit.

The former World War II cameraman who had helped film the Nurenberg War Crimes trials walked out of the large two-square-block company building and glanced overhead. Dark clouds threatened.

But then, he saw something else.

Moving at perhaps no more than 25 m.p.h. was an immense object about 1,000 feet overhead that James thought was a zeppelin, but it surely was infinitely larger than the Hindenberg, which he had seen one time when he was a kid. The massive structure stretched at least 1,000 feet from tip to stern, he estimated, and must have been as big around as a building, perhaps 130 feet or so on a side, for maybe a total of 400 feet around. It had no tail fins, but was rounded on the back, like a donut, from which he could see heat escaping. He did not see any markings or identifying insig-

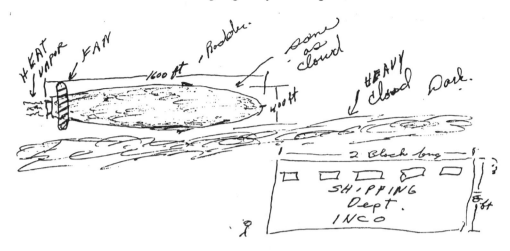

nia on its dull gray surface. There appeared to be no external gondola or other apparatus (see above drawing).

James could hear a slight humming sound, and thought maybe there was an internal jet engine hidden somewhere in the massive hull.

"I call it an airship, but I don't know what it was," he says.

He watched the ship for perhaps a minute in all before it disappeared over the hill in the direction of the approaching storm.

He says another man in another part of town saw the same thing, and that it was later reported in the local paper.

After his sighting, James wrote to Arthur R. Bink, an airship historian, for an opinion. Mr. Bink's response follows.

Arthur R. Bink
airship historian,
advanced collector of airship memorabilia

write: Zeppelin
P.O. Box 2502
Cinnaminson, NJ 08077 USA

January 2, 1994

Dear James,

Thank you for your letter and drawing. I'm not quite sure what to make of your experience, but I'm afraid I can't shed any light on it. It sounds like more of a UFO item than a zeppelin, dirigible, airship, or blimp item. Airships have small motors along their sides, rather than the large jet-like exhaust shown in your picture. An airship of any size usually has 4 fins in the rear, some shaped like a cross, and others are shaped like an "X". Some early airships had only 3 fins, and one had as many as 10 fins arranged in a circle. The largest airship ever produced was 805 feet long, and was 135 feet in diameter. Ninety-nine percent of them had multiple engines, and you could hear the engines 'talk' to one another because of the harmonics set up when some are running just a little faster than others. Also, airships are relatively slow, and wouldn't 'disappear' by the time you ran around from the front of a building to the rear. Airships of today normally cruise at only 35 miles per hour, but can go up to 55 if pressed. They are by law required to fly no lower than 1000 feet, except when over water; it sounds like whatever you saw was flying quite a bit lower than that. You didn't mention what kind of sounds it was making, for example the engines, etc.

At any rate, I'm afraid I can't help you, especially since I wasn't there and didn't see it. If you ever see it again or find out more about it, I'd be interested in hearing from you. Better yet, if you can photograph it using a camera or a camcorder, that would be excellent.

Thanks for writing. Good luck in your research.

Very truly yours,
Arthur R. Bink
NAVY LAKE HURST HISTORICAL SOCIETY
(Trustee and Relics Custodian)
NAVAL AIRSHIP ASSOCIATION
GOODYEAR BLIMP CLUB
LIGHTER-THAN-AIR SOCIETY
AERIAL AMBASSADORS CLUB
AEROPHILATELIC FEDERATION OF THE AMERICAS
ZEPPELIN COLLECTORS CLUB

1992

Stanley (not his real name) is a successful Morgantown businessman with more questions than answers about UFOs.

One afternoon, after having just driven up the on-ramp to I-68 from Rt. 857 near Cheat Lake, Stanley and his son, who was attending WVU law school at the time, spotted "a silvery, almost translucent object of enormous size behind Raese Mansion," a local landmark (see drawing, next page).

"At first, I thought it was a plane crashing," Stanley says, because the

object appeared to be going down at a steep angle.

"It had a definite shape and texture, like a glass test-tube," he says. "I kept driving towards the hill behind which the object had disappeared, but it did not reappear."

He says at least two cars were parked alongside I-68 and that their occupants had to be watching the same thing.

Ten seconds passed, and still the object had not reappeared from the narrow gorge where it had gone. Passing by the spot, the men looked, but could not see it—anywhere.

"We looked at each other," Stanley says, "and we said, 'Did you see that?' We saw the same thing."

Stanley exited onto the Pierpont Road and called the airport to inquire about any plane crashes or may-day reports, but was told that all was quiet.

The men then returned home. "My memory of this is very vivid," Stanley remarks, "when we came home it was very important to me that we separate and draw this thing. We did that, and the drawings were the same, on the same scale."

"The memory began dissipating immediately and was not as vivid after that. And I'm always questioning now, did I actually see this?"

1994

Angie B. (a pseudonym), 17, a junior at the Montcalm High School

143

near Bluefield (Mercer County), her brother, mother and a friend watched through binoculars some round objects performing strange maneuvers over an abandoned air strip for three hours one night in July.

"My mom now denies that she saw it," Angie says, "because she doesn't want to believe they're anything out of the ordinary. But I know they weren't jets or planes, 'cause they didn't make any noise."

Angie admits that she was skeptical at first, too, but as they continued watching, "It scared the hell out of me."

She recalls seeing similar aerobatics on "almost every clear night for the past year," but says the objects were closer this night than ever before.

1993

Tricia Melvin-Somerville at her farm. Photo by Bob Teets.

One summer night about 10:30 p.m. while on her way to work at the Greenbrier Valley Medical Center in Lewisburg (Greenbrier County), R.N. Tricia Melvin-Somerville "heard something that I assumed was a plane, a motor sound...way up there."

Next thing she knew, it was right over top of her Porsche 911, shinning an incredibly bright spotlight down on her. "From what I could tell, it was round," she says. "And as wide as seven cars."

Tricia, who races vintage sports cars on weekend circuits, punched the 911's accelerator and yelled, "Don't pick me up!"

In seconds, the Porsche was going 110 m.p.h. down Rt. 12—

—but the light stayed right with her.

"They were doing it on purpose," she says. "And I was scared."

The chase lasted several minutes, and just as Tricia was beginning to sense terror— "Suddenly, up it goes!"

The light disappeared in a flash, "straight up."

She says now she can't understand why, given the speed she was driving, she arrived five to ten minutes late for work.

1994

Lucy Q. (not her real name), 26, and her boyfriend, Richard B. (a pseudonym), were taking an evening ride around Morgantown, Monongalia County, on February 20.

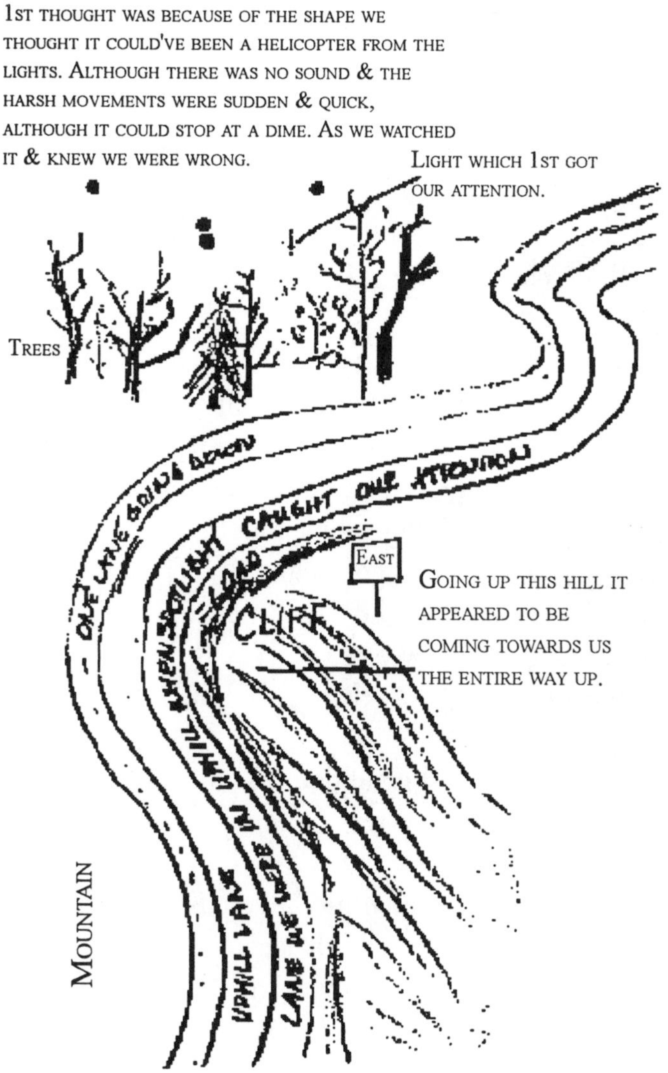

1ST THOUGHT WAS BECAUSE OF THE SHAPE WE THOUGHT IT COULD'VE BEEN A HELICOPTER FROM THE LIGHTS. ALTHOUGH THERE WAS NO SOUND & THE HARSH MOVEMENTS WERE SUDDEN & QUICK, ALTHOUGH IT COULD STOP AT A DIME. AS WE WATCHED IT & KNEW WE WERE WRONG.

LIGHT WHICH 1ST GOT OUR ATTENTION.

TREES

OUR LANE GOING DOWN

CAUGHT OUR ATTENTION

ROAD

DOWNHILL WHEN IT

EAST

CLIFF

GOING UP THIS HILL IT APPEARED TO BE COMING TOWARDS US THE ENTIRE WAY UP.

LANE WE WERE IN WHILE

UPHILL LANE

MOUNTAIN

Lucy: We were headed up the hill on University Avenue (see drawing at left), east, towards the Ramada Inn. The windows were down just a little bit. It was probably about 9:45 p.m. We cruise around every night, before he takes me home. Up ahead...was a real bright light. You couldn't help yourself but to see it. Anybody would see it, although it looked like it was a helicopter. Beaming down, like looking for a fugitive or something. They were real close to these two homes that are right up there on the mountain.

Richard said, "That looks like a helicopter."

I said it wasn't, and the beam went off and then it came back on again. The funny thing about the light, it's like a beam. A light that has no rays, it was a big light and it made a big light down below on the ground.

Finally, as we're getting towards it, he says, "Lucy, that's not a helicopter." It's sitting still and barely moving and we heard nothing.

As we got closer, we saw three lights shaped like in a triangle. Actually there were four but we couldn't see the back one.

He said, "That can't be a plane, I don't know what that is. Surely, that's not a helicopter."

So, we're on the side of it now and it's just coming right along with us. There was nothing there. Just a big huge gully, big valley. As we go around a curve, heading towards a stoplight next to the Ramada Inn, the thing starts crossing over the top of us. At that time, there were four lights on it and it was square.

Soon as we went through that stop light, there was that thing. I mean right on top of us. Awesome, and flat, it was flat. I said, "I swear to God it's a UFO! It's a UFO!" He says, "I know, I know it's a UFO!"

He's terrified. I wanted to go see, like follow it. He didn't want to, he was terrified. I got him to get on the highway at least, headed back towards Morgantown.

Okay, it was flying along and the thing completely turned on its side. It was flat...It was a perfect square. No noise, we weren't really moving fast and there were really no cars on the highway. For a split second, it just sat there. I felt like it wanted us to see. Like it was showing off. I could see ridges and seams. Like if you start welding metal together, or trying to melt aluminum cans together, you have a jagged seam all different shapes and sizes. It was like a whitish gray color and it was brushed, like brushed aluminum. It's not of any metal that I've ever seen. It was almost as if it was cement, I don't know what it was. It was there for about a second, on its side. And it was huge, it was real big.

We're here on the highway and all of a sudden it zooms off.

It went towards Fairmont. It was 10:10 p.m. when we saw it.

Then, as we headed back to Morgantown, we saw it again, hovering. If we had gone south towards Fairmont, we would have passed it again. It wasn't high in the sky at all. It was where you might see a hospital helicopter. Very low. No sound. We didn't see a spot where this light came from. That's what freaked him out the most.

When we hit the exit Richard was flying.

I called the airport. The man who answered said, "I'll tell you, had nothing in that area at 10:10. Let me call Charleston." He talks to them, I can hear him...he explained it to them. He asked about it, how high, etcetera, said it must have been too low to be picked up on our radar. They both said there was nothing near that area anywhere. I knew I had something then.

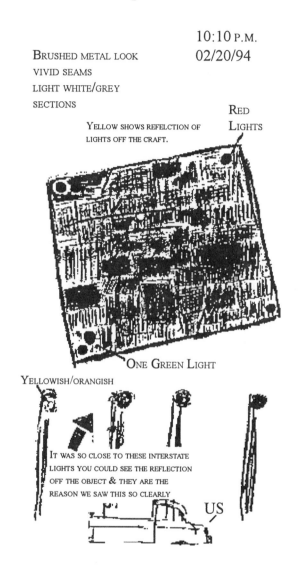

10:10 P.M.
02/20/94

BRUSHED METAL LOOK
VIVID SEAMS
LIGHT WHITE/GREY
SECTIONS

RED LIGHTS

YELLOW SHOWS REFELCTION OF LIGHTS OFF THE CRAFT.

ONE GREEN LIGHT

YELLOWISH/ORANGISH

IT WAS SO CLOSE TO THESE INTERSTATE LIGHTS YOU COULD SEE THE REFLECTION OFF THE OBJECT & THEY ARE THE REASON WE SAW THIS SO CLEARLY

US

B: Did you sense intelligence on board it?

L: I didn't think any of that, really. We were just shocked. Until I called...then I thought yes, something had to be controlling it.

B: Have any unusual thoughts?

L: I was never afraid. He was terrified. I don't why I wasn't afraid. I can't explain it.

B: Did it attempt to communicate with you in some way?

L: No, I'm just...I just don't get scared. I can accept things, I have an open mind. He grew up differently, watched scary stuff on TV and he's so much more afraid...He's scared they will come and get him. He truly believes that there are UFOs and aliens out there. Like the government is holding something back. Now that I've seen one, I'm sure there's other life forms out there. I know that what I saw was not of this earth, at all. I don't think our people can design a machine that goes through the sky, maneuvers like it does and is silent. My father helps design aircraft, and worked on designing the Douglass DC10, so I'm familiar with about anything that flies. It's got to be from somewhere else.

B: Did you believe there were "aliens" before you saw this?

L: No.

B: But you did afterwards?

L: Yes. Somebody, beings, I don't know if they're aliens. A month ago, I was driving up behind the new mall here. Richard was with me, trying out my 4-wheel-drive. There was something up in the sky and there was like five different things around it like they were just keeping up with it. It just flew over top of us. I know there's stuff out there and the military is keeping stuff secret. The fifth thing was in the middle and there were four things around it. You could hear them. It was too high up to tell what it was. It was going so slow, you couldn't believe it.

B: Do you feel special?

L: I think if it goes around picking people...some people think they come to certain individuals for whatever reason, I think they came to the right person, because I have a real big mouth. It's doesn't affect me if people say I'm crazy. I tell them what I saw.

I really feel these things are going to land on this earth. Land somewhere, get out and just starting walking around.

1994

Floyd P. (not his real name), 72, is retired and lives in Spencer (Roane County).

On June 24, 1994, he walked outside his house to discover that a roisterous thunderstorm was approaching.

Suddenly, an 8- to 12-foot round craft shot out of a bank of large, dark clouds and flew directly over him about 500 feet on a straight course to the southeast.

"The front one-third of it" gleamed like a mirror, "and the back two-thirds was dark gray." There was no rotor, no protrusions at all, but once, for less than a second, he thought he saw a reflection of a "small, transparent wing." Otherwise, the object was perfectly round.

He watched it proceed for about a mile before he lost sight of it.

"I was amazed," he says. "But there's a lot more to be seen. I believe these things will happen and that a major part of the people will be deceived by this. I expect more of these flying things to appear."

When I ask about his religious views, he responds cautiously.

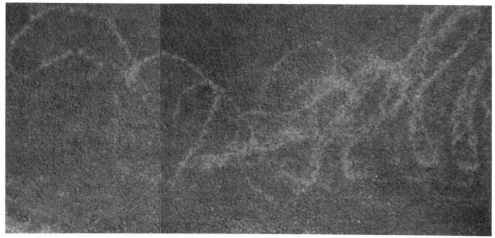

A combination of two of "Floyd's" photographs reveals the strange markings he found in his yard, which he calls "snake-tracks." He claims to know of no cause for the markings, having discounted obvious ones (moles, etc.).

"I try to abide by God's rules and regulations. According to Him, He didn't create beings any more intelligent than us. I believe there is some kind of flying vehicle out there, but where it comes from, I won't make a statement on that."

Floyd says his father used to see mysterious lights, which old-timers back then used to refer to as "jack-o-lanterns." His older brother once "saw a whole hillside full of 'em on the family farm about 12 to 14 miles west toward Ripley" he says.

Floyd is worried that the government may be interested in his sighting, so he asks that I not use his name.

(Note: His reference to "jack-o-lanterns" has been repeated to me often by many callers from the Ripley area, a place where there is definitely something going on, as it has for generations.)

1990

"It was huge."

Gregg B. Knight was talking with an old man named Brian L. (a pseudonym) outside of the latter's son-in-law's mobile home in Belmont (Pleasants County). "Brian is a very mentally disturbed individual," says Gregg, "who quit work because of events in his life and in his daughter's life in Louisiana because of contacts with aliens."

It was a clear afternoon, warm enough that the men needed only light

Gregg B. Knight worked with artist Nancy Summers to assure he had an accurate depiction of his 1990 sighting in Belmont. The above is a scanned and much reduced reproduction of the very large original.

outerwear to be comfortable.

Despite his mental problems, Brian is, according to Gregg, "very, very knowledgeable about the Bible. He has followed the life of Jesus as well as any ordained minister. But he wasn't into shoving it down your throat.

"I asked him, I said, 'If I ask my Dad a question, he answers. If I ask God the Father something, he won't answer, sometimes for years. Now why is that?'

"'It depends on what you ask,' Brian answered.

"And I said, 'Like UFOs, what could they be? I want to see an alien craft not of this world.'"

"And he said, 'Look there.'"

Gregg looked toward the west, and the sight "took my breath away."

It was a massive craft, so huge it "blocked out the sun, and yet it didn't cast a shadow." Gregg estimates it was more than 2,000 feet in length, with a finish like that of "a Chrysler 426 hemi engine, that's it exactly." Its features resembled "a battleship turned upside down."

"I yelled for my wife as loud as I could, or at least I thought I did," he recalls, "but no one came out."

After it was gone, Gregg looked at Brian. "Did you see that!" he asked, incredulously.

"Sure," Brian answered. "That ain't nothing, that's just a mother ship. You ought to see a colony ship. And then wait 'til you talk to 'em."

Gregg says Brian's son, who was 20 miles away in Parkersburg, saw it too. From his perspective, it appeared to be about the size of a baseball on the horizon.

It was Gregg's sighting which led him to become interested in MUFON, the Mutual UFO Network, Inc., an international nonprofit organization which attempts to examine UFO phenomena through local volunteer "field investigators" in all 50 states, Canada and many other countries.

Gregg now serves as MUFON Assistant State Director for West Virginia, and has investigated dozens of cases. His day job is as a deputy for the Harrison County Police Department.

"I just wish I could have a sighting everyday," he says, reflecting on his momentous Belmont sighting.

Even though he has read in books and heard from contactees that "some beings are good, and some are bad," he still insists that, "I want to have contact. Somebody knew what I wanted the Belmont sighting, as if it were planned. It confirmed in my mind that they're there when I need 'em. I would try to protect them if they contacted me, to see what I could do for them. I want to hear what they have to say."

1990 (Letter Excerpt):

(Note: Marvin is retired, 62 years old)
   I am very happy to share this (*see drawings on this and next page*) with you. I would not take anything for what I saw and I'm sure my sister feels the same way. We are looking for-

NIGHT SKY ABOUT 10:30 P.M. OCT. 1990

OTHER TREES ON RIDGE ¼ MILE AWAY.

ORANGE LIGHT WITH NO BEAM JUST A STEADY GLOW, 3' TO 4' IN DIAMETER

TREES NEAR SIDE

UNDER GROWTH

I-64, THE OTHER ROW OF TREES AND RIVER ON THE OTHER SIDE OF THESE TREES. THE AREA AROUND THE LIGHT APPEARED TO BE A LITTLE DARKER THAN THE BACKGROUND BUT I COULD NOT MAKE OUT AN EXACT SHAPE.

ward to the next sighting and we may never see another in our lifetime. It sure is a great feeling.

On July 14, 1994 my wife and I were coming home from Charleston, and on my radio we were listening to Chuck Carter who has a talk show. A woman called in and told him that a triangular-shaped UFO was over her parked vehicle, it had lights all over it, they just glowed and had no beams. Her two dogs got scared and ran in the house. She said that since this en-

Marvin R. Smith's Sighting (Two Drawings)

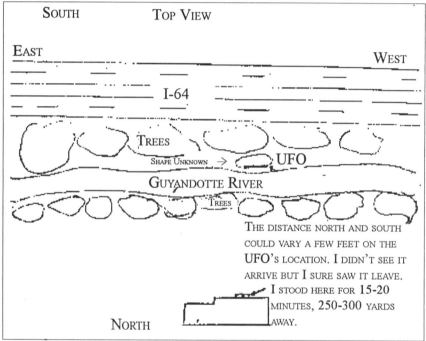

SOUTH   TOP VIEW

EAST   WEST

I-64

TREES

SHAPE UNKNOWN → UFO

GUYANDOTTE RIVER

TREES

THE DISTANCE NORTH AND SOUTH COULD VARY A FEW FEET ON THE UFO'S LOCATION. I DIDN'T SEE IT ARRIVE BUT I SURE SAW IT LEAVE. I STOOD HERE FOR 15-20 MINUTES, 250-300 YARDS AWAY.

NORTH

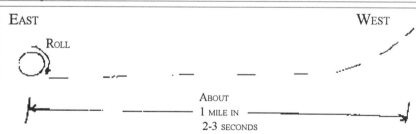

EAST   WEST

ROLL

ABOUT 1 MILE IN 2-3 SECONDS

IT ROLLED TO MY RIGHT ABOUT 15° AND THE BLACK MASS WENT TO WITH IT AND I STILL COULD NOT MAKE OUT IT'S SHAPE AND THEN IT WAS GONE SO FAST IT APPEARED TO HAVE A TAIL SEVERAL HUNDRED FEET LONG. IT WAS PLAYING A TRICK ON MY EYES. NO SOUND AT ANY TIME.

Marvin R. Smith's Sister's Sighting (Three Drawings)

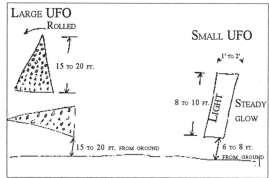

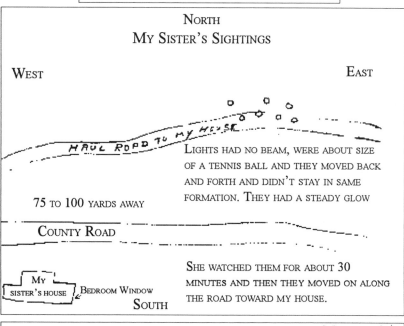

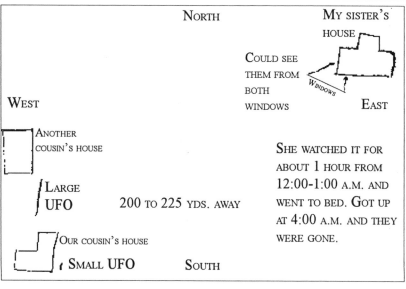

counter she has felt very weak. Her doctor could not find anything wrong with her.

This is the same shape my sister saw.

Marvin L. Smith
Huntington, WV

1994 (Letter Excerpt):

"The front left light was red. The front right light was white. The back one was green. They blinked on and off in a pattern. It went like this: the front two—then it went the front two again. Then all three blinked at the same time. But when the front two blinked on, the red blinked on, then the white.

"The object, UFO, or ship from outer space did the pattern twice before it flew out of sight. It flew pretty low, probably between 5,000 and 10,000 feet. When it flew over I heard nothing but the neighbors and crickets. I saw it because it was dusk and I went outside for some air. When I saw it (*see drawing above*) my mind went blank. I saw it for about five seconds.

"After I saw it, I ran in the house and told my family I saw a UFO. But they said I was full of it except my little brother Ryan Beasley. He said he would go outside with me and see if we could see it or anything else out of the ordinary. We saw nothing but shooting stars. This was early to mid August, 1994. When I came back in, I thought it was odd 'cause what I saw was kind of heart-shaped, made no sound, and went about 100 to 200 m.p.h. faster than the average airplane. So I took out my Desert Storm cards to see if I could see one that would even look a little like what I saw. No luck.

"I will look and see if I can see that object again. Like quoted in the beginning of the *X-Files* 'The truth is out there.'"

Jeremy Beasley
Age 13
Clay, WV

July 3, 1994

It was a curious day, indeed. At least five people in West Virginia saw a UFO on July 3, 1994, and from their descriptions, it would seem at least four saw the same one. One of the people, "Daniel" (whose story appears on Page 24) believes he was visited by aliens that day at his store. Sandra Holmes (whose other experiences are shared on Page 109), and three Morgantown men, all neighbors, saw similar objects.

Eighty-one-year-old Steve Kudla stands on his porch. The object he saw (see drawing) appeared in the northern sky which, in the photo, appears above and behind Steve's left shoulder.

At 10:30 p.m., 81-year-old Steve Kudla sat on his porch watching a fireworks display occurring west of his home and across the valley at the Morgantown Mall. Looking north for a second, he noticed a curious white light moving back and forth (see drawing, below). As he continued watching, it "tilted and I could see six more lights in a circle, then four dropped down."

Jim Kinsley, who lives in a house just below Steve's, saw something "brighter than the North Star moving from north to south before the fireworks. It stopped over in the west, an abrupt stop," he says.

Jim, as well as Steve, have had other sightings and unusual experiences.

Ralph Morris, in his house across from Steve's, saw "a real bright light toward the north, about the size of a softball." This was before the fireworks started. "I meant to mention it to someone a lot of friends were gathered in his yard preparing to watch the fireworks across the valley, but I just didn't say anything about it. It was an awful bright star, and I've never seen one that bright nor that big, either."

On her way home at about 11:45 p.m., Sandra Holmes saw something unusual.

"I saw something coming across the mountains to the northeast. It looked like a strobe light, reflective lights on it. Very bright and it pulsated. When it got brighter, an opening appeared in it that was black.

BLACK M
BRIGHTEST INTEN.

Sandra Holmes' drawing of her July 3, 1994 sighting.

The object Steve Kudla saw from his porch on July 3, 1994. Drawing by Bob Teets.

"I pulled off and watched it. I rolled down the window. No sound, but if there was a sound, it was a *click*. Like a camera shutter *click*, maybe. It was pulsating in the same pattern, like...*bright-dim-bright* ...that's what caught my attention."

Flashback to the 70's

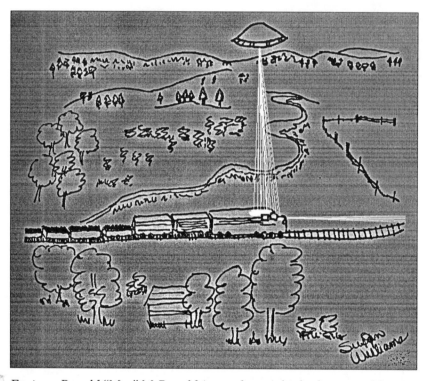

Engineer Donald "Mac" McDonald (a pseudonym), his brakeman and fireman were headed down the famous 17-mile grade out of West Virginia and into Maryland with 10,000 tons of coal behind them in a hundred-car train back one night in '75. Everything was going smoothly when suddenly, "a bright, blinding light hit us from overhead," Mac says. Though the men tried, they could not see the light's source concealed behind the brilliant glare. "It wasn't a helicopter," Mac states, "because there was no noise." The mysterious light stayed with the advancing train for perhaps four or five minutes before it disappeared. "I suspect it was a secret military craft of some kind, what with the Cold War and all," Mac, who now lives in Preston County, comments. "'Course, it could have been a flying saucer, too. I have no knowledge of either one." He says the trio never reported their sighting because it would have drawn "horse-laughs" from their fellow workers— and suspicious stares from their boss. Drawing by Terra Alta artist Susan Williams.

Stonewood (Harrison County) resident Karen Heaster is a MUFON investigator with plenty of sightings of her own. Here's a sampling:

Karen: I saw beautiful lights coming up over the hill. I thought, "Wow, a show plane." I got in my Bronco and drove off. About three weeks later I saw it again (*see drawing at left*). I noticed it had two rings, consisting of red, green and white lights alternating evenly. I called Jackson's Mill airport, they reported no such traffic. Weston said no, never seen anything like this; so did Benedum in Clarksburg.

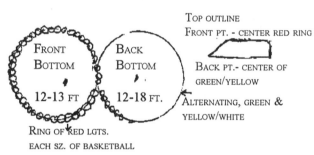

On September 17, 1993, my twin was in from CA. We were sitting on the front stoop. Here came the show plane. It moved from west to east, it was the most beautiful thing I've ever seen and it was right above my house. It was awesome, so huge but it had a humming engine.

Bob: Did you have any thoughts external to your own?

K: Almost like the first time it let me see a glimpse, second time a glimpse, the third time it was like, "You're okay, I'm going to let you see me."

I didn't feel fear, it was awe. The top, the cab-part of it, appeared be a dark...like a brassy gold, like a dirty brass. We could see in detail, that's why we don't understand why we didn't put the binoculars up because we're sure we could've seen something inside of it. It was that close. The external feelings were good vibes. No fear at all.

B: Did you feel as if there was intelligence on board?

K: Definitely. It was a friendly feeling. It was almost like we had met them before.

B: Where do you think this intelligence came from?

K: I believe it's coming from underground, right here on earth. This particular one. After checking with airports, coming always from the same place behind the hill where there are abandoned mines partially filled with water. It always comes at the same angle.

B: You think it's staying in one of the mines?

K: Yes. More and more I have that belief. It had no landing gear. If it were to set down, it would have broken all of those huge, basketball size lights that were making the rings.

B: Where did it go?

K: East, traveling very slow. Came out of the west at the Gocke Mines and headed east. It was very slow, it started ascending, gained its altitude and then picked up speed. Cleared the top of the hill and we haven't seen it again to this day.

We feel it controlled us in keeping my sister with the binoculars in her hands, I with a camcorder, my husband beside me with a 35 mm camera loaded right inside a door. It gave us plenty of chance to do it. But not one of us did. It was like, "You can see me, but I'll never let you take a picture." I long to see this one again.

B: Tell me about the arch.

K: I call it one half of the "McDonalds Arch." This came out of the east, heading north around the hill. It arched around the hill, it looked like a car driving around the hill. No distinct lights, but the front was amber, a very dark amber. The inside was a glowing gold, the most beautiful glowing gold I've ever seen. As it moved on around it was almost like it was only for me even though other people were watching it, too. Nobody else could see it.

She (the neighbor) said, "Look at the amber light." I looked up and saw it. They saw the amber light, but when it actually got into the form, to where I saw the arch, it became the most brilliant gold I have ever seen. No noise at all. Just like floating, like an angel-type floating. When it went, there were no blinking lights, no sound.

I was so exhausted, I didn't want to go up there to watch with them.

B: Exhausted from what?

K: The work of the day. I went just to please them. However, after it went slowly around the hill, I felt a spiritual connection to it. It's almost like when you go to a church service and come out feeling like your cup was turned up and overflowing rather than turned down. I can't say it was a religious, spiritual connection, but it was a peaceful, totally peaceful connection.

It was like I had taken something to calm me totally down. My back quit hurting, I was no longer tired and sleepy. It was like I didn't have a worry in the world. At this time my husband was involved in a strike, we did have a lot of worries. My father had been sick and I was taking care of him, running two homes.

It was like nothing mattered, nothing existed.

B: The feelings were external and coming from this object, so you attribute intelligence to this one as well?

K: Absolutely. It was almost like, "I want to help you. I want to take away any stress you feel." I even consulted a local psychiatrist, told him what I'd seen and felt. He agreed with me that the reason the others didn't feel it was because their lives were okay.

Then perhaps, about three weeks later I was extremely upset because by this time I'm totally weird. I'm running two homes, taking care of my father who is totally dependent on me, and in the middle of all this mess, I found out I had a serious health problem. I didn't know how much more I could take.

I went out and sat on the front steps by myself and I told David (her husband) I needed to be left alone for a while.

And the Arch returned, came out of the east and made an arch toward the west, and back towards the north again.

It was almost like it was draining me of my fatigue and my worry. It was like, "You've made it this far, you're going to make it the rest of the way. Everything's going to work out." Again, I had this total peace.

I went in, kissed everybody good night, went over to Dad's, slept the night beautifully. Woke up the next day totally refreshed. It was as if it had taken away any thoughts of my ownself. Instead of being self-absorbed, whatever this is, is very good for me.

B: Did it seem to help your health problem?

K: It didn't heal it, but it let the medical doctors finally come to an agreement. It sent me in the direction to get help.

B: You attribute that to this sighting?

K: Absolutely.

The strange part was, my father became less dependent, we went back to work from the strike, my health problems improved, it was almost like it solved some of my personal problems.

B: You have described this as almost angelic in nature.

K: Absolutely.

B: Do you think it's an angel?

K: I think it could be angelic like, due to the fact it doesn't want anybody to see it unless you're having problems. If your life is in order, at the moment, you don't see it.

It could be an angel, but what I see is solid, it's something like I could touch. I long to see it again. Even in my sleep, I'll see it. It calms me to this day.

B: Why do you think this chose you?

K: Because of my belief in my family, God and prayer. I knew that a lot of my family and friends were praying for me and my situation. I feel that it was because of the faith of others. So yes, I connect prayer to this.

It was like somebody had given me a good energy shot.

We turn now to some of Karen's case files. All those whose names appear have granted permission to do so.

Cheryl
UFO Sighting, 8 April 1994, 2340 hrs.
Suds Run Community, near Quiet Dell, WV, Harrison, USA

"My nephews and I were traveling down Suds Run Road shortly before midnight on April 8, 1994.

"Looking ahead, we saw a bright red light with reflection on the trees moving from behind the hill on our left. We thought is was an airplane at first, but when more of the lights was exposed, we knew that it was not.

"The object was clearly circular and appearing to be dark, like badly tarnished silver. We all noticed a diamond-shaped window in the center side and also, it made no sound.

"I was traveling at about 30 m.p.h. and backed off the speed so as to observe it. It traveled across the road in front of us at 300 to 500 feet, so we were able to see it clearly. At this time it lowered its altitude. It went to the

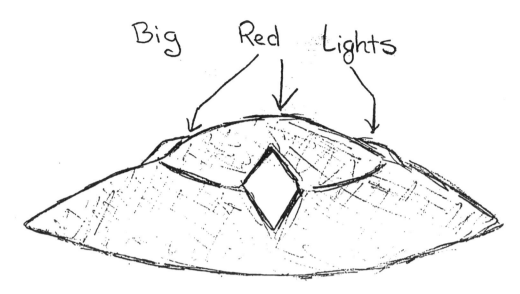

opposite side of the road, to another hill and started ascending as if to go over it. However, when it reached the top of the trees, it stopped for a second and slowly came back down.

"When it reached the top of the hill, my radio started screeching and the tape in the tape deck literally began rattling. The object seemed to go the same speed we were but when my car acted as though it might stall, I became frightened and headed for Route 20 South as fast as I could.

"When we arrived at Anmore, I noticed my clock had been erased and the rest of my dash lights were very dim. The lights were fine the next morning.

"I always said that I would not believe in UFOs until I saw one with my own eyes. We are now believers!!!

"I was told by a friend to call Mrs. Heaster, which my 16-year-old nephew did, shortly after midnight."

Cheryl Allen, age 39

Jacqueline M. Jordon
October 15, 1993
8 p.m.

"I was in my car going down Cost Ave. in Stonewood and saw in the sky ahead of me in the NE a red and green and white dot in the sky. I went to my friend's house in Chestnut Hills, Clarksburg, to see if it was like the one they had seen a couple of weeks before.

"When I arrived at their house, we observed one in the north with a

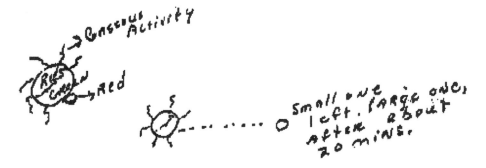

small light at the bottom right of it. The small red light moved slowly away from the big one to the right. We decided to go to (Name's) parents to get a high powered scope so we could view it better. It was still in the north but as we left Broad Oaks, the small one seemed to move slowly back to the big one. Before we reached (Name) and (Name's) home it disappeared. Not one of us could say where it went.

"It was really interesting, but I know it was not a star or planet unless they have decided to start moving and spitting out little ones."

Linda Dorsey

"One evening October 1, 1993, my husband and I were driving down Route 98 from Nutter Fort and saw an object coming from the North. It seemed to reach the area in front of us and follow the car. It was awesome in appearance, much like the one we observed with Jackie but was much closer. This 'following' continued almost the length of Rt. 98 to Chestnut St. then it went away so fast, it appeared to have never been in front of us.

"I don't know where it went, as we had no obstructions in the area of the sky we were viewing, but I know one thing, it was not a plane, or tower lights, etc.

"I am now a believer and will never forget what I saw. I have not been fortunate enough to see anything unusual since then, not that they are not there, perhaps I have not had the time to watch the sky with a new baby to give all my attention."

Linda Dorsey, Clarksburg, WV

Anonymous
October 24, 1993 in the p.m. Saw it for 3 to 5 minutes.
"I was standing in my yard looking at the sky. I saw a large unusual

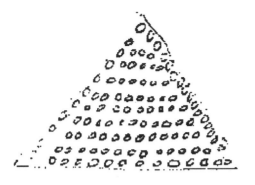

lighted object flying over me and it made no noise. I thought it was a plane.

"I just stood and watched it, trying to figure out what it was. I told my friends about it 10 minutes later.

"It looked like the shape of a stealth bomber with white light all over the bottom of it. The lights didn't blink. They stayed on like car headlights. It moved slowly across the sky in a straight line. I don't know how I lost sight of it."

Adult

October 15, 1993—Nutter Fort, across the river from Karen Heaster.

"On the evening of Oct. 15 there were objects flying over my house in Nutter Fort. Some of these flying objects had white lights and some had red and green lights. They would move quickly through the sky—disappear and appear again in another part of the sky. I think they moved too quick to be an airplane or helicopter."

Karen Heaster
Nov. 10, 1993

"On November 10, 1993 in the p.m. I was standing on my front porch talking on the phone to a friend. I saw coming across the sky a goldish-

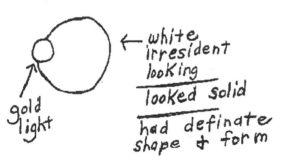

white flying saucer. I had this object in my sight for 45 seconds. It was traveling approximately 25 to 30 m.p.h. My friend took her portable phone, went outside to try and see the saucer but could not see it from her location. While still talking to her I stated that I was going to take a picture of it. I rushed inside and got my camera which I keep beside the door. I took three pictures of the saucer. The pictures have been developed and all three show the saucer. I watched the saucer until it went out of sight."

163

Child

Oct. 13, 1993— 12 or 13 years old.

"I have always believed in UFOs. I'm a firm believer. The first time I saw a UFO was when I was visiting with Mrs. (Name's) daughter (Name). They had photos and a video tape of the UFOs and were taking them to an expert photographer who was a friend of theirs.

"When we got there I looked at the photos and watched a little bit of the video, so did the photographer. He didn't really say anything, at first he just made up excuses. Then me and (Name) went out on the porch to talk. After a while I decided to look for a UFO, so I got up and walked out on their sidewalk and looked up. Suddenly, I saw a star that appeared to be moving, then I saw it move. This time I was sure. Then I thought, probably an airplane, but then it made a sharp turn and started zigzagging and then stopped. Then it would start up again.

"I pointed to the sky and said "Hey, (Name)! Is that a UFO?" She said, "I don't know, I can't see from over here." So I go in the house and have everyone come out to see it, and quickly go back to the sidewalk to find it again. When they got beside me I pointed to the sky and said, "Right there."

"Yep," said Mrs. (Name), "that's a UFO."

"Then everyone else spotted it but the photographer. He was still making up excuses, saying it was a plane, but soon changed his mind when he saw it making zigzags. After that, I spotted many more, all together I've seen about eleven up 'til now.

"There was one time when it was around 10 p.m. and I was upstairs praying. I turned and faced the window and saw blue, red and white lights flashing like light bulbs one after the other. It couldn't have been a plane. For one thing, plane lights make a triangle and don't blink, for another they don't stay in one spot, and for another they don't take off straight up in the air.

"My brother didn't believe me until a couple of days ago. I showed him one when we were on the school bus, and now he believes me.

"They are mostly found by a bunch of stars or a constellation like the Big Dipper. You have to look at the sky very closely or you won't be able to spot one. They look like stars or up closer they have white, red and blue flashing lights. Their movements consist of zigzagging, circling, sharp turns, making square patterns, standing still, or going straight up or down. Sometimes they seem to fall straight down like a shooting star, but don't have a tail, only a head."

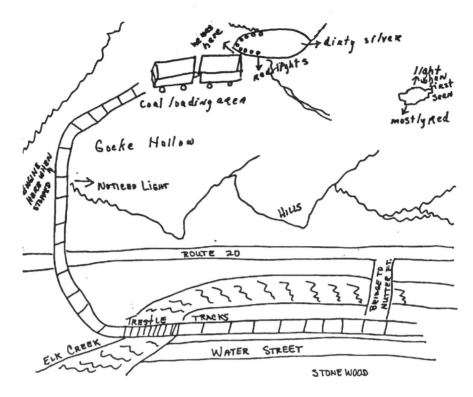

The "Train Story" As told to Karen Heaster by Mrs. (Name):

"It was 1954, when the trains still ran into Gocke Hollow to pick up coal and bring it to the tipple located on Water Street in Stonewood, WV.

"On this particular evening, October as I remember, my husband left for work as usual. His job was to ride the back car of the train and signal the engineer as it backed into the hollow to load the first coal of the cat-eye shift.

"The next day, he returned home from work, white-faced as could be, and told me the following story:

"He climbed up on the side rail of the last car, swung his light to signal the engineer that he was ready.

"The cars started to back slowly up the track, across the trestle which exists today. As the car passed the trestle and entered the first curve of track, he noticed a small-like light deep into the hollow. As the train moved, the light grew larger. Watching the light and the track at the same time, he noticed that it had distinct shape...rather oval, with lights across the front.

"When the train neared its stopping point, the object hovered, lights blinking. Due to the length of the cars, he could not signal the engineer of what he was seeing. At this time, the object moved over the train, the length of which covered two rail cars and the width was about 25 feet. He

165

held to the side of the car as tight as he could, fear overtaking him. A few seconds later he tried to get down and could not move. At the same time, he smelled burning coal.

"When the cars were emptied at the tipple, some bug-dust and small pieces of coal remained and this is what was on fire. The heat from the object had set it on fire and the cars were beginning to smell hot.

"The engineer tried to look for a signal to find the reason for the bright light, but got no response. Not wanting to leave his engine, he decided to wait until he got a signal or the man himself came to him.

"Finally, the object left, straight up, and disappeared. After a few `minutes, he was able to jump from the car, but felt sick and weak. He made it to the engine and told his story to the engineer, who laughed at him until he noticed the glove on his left hand was almost burned from his fingers.

"He moved the train out of the hollow to a house on the other side of the trestle, each promising the other they would never tell what really happened. Rather than to allow the engineer to take him home, he stayed at the home until end of shift and allowed the lady of the house to dress his hand.

"He went to his grave having nightmares and would never ride the train on cat-eye again."

(NOTE: This lady died 12/20/93)

Hayhursts, Kenneth Scheuvront

"While standing on my front porch I saw a red, white and green lighted flying object in the sky. It was traveling northwest at an even rate of speed that I would estimate at 35 mph. As it got to a location above Maple Avenue, it came to an almost complete stop. This object looked like it had applied its brakes just like we do when we drive a car. The object made a turn to the north at a 45-degree angle. *This object looked like it had come to a city corner and made a right turn!* I didn't hear any noise coming from this object."

Kenneth Scheuvront
Summer 1976

"At Gregory's Run (near Wilsonburg Rt. 50 West of Clarksburg) sitting on the front porch when suddenly the object appeared, football field in size, red in color, oblong diamond shape—brilliant in color. I have never seen anything like it before and was unable to identify it as anything familiar to me. It hovered approximately 100' off the ground. I heard what

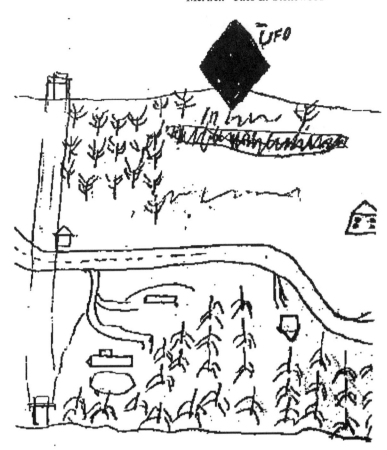

sounded like a shotgun blast and when it was apparently hit, a bright flash occurred and the object immediately ascended, at a moderate speed at first, then rapidly disappeared.

"For the next three weeks after the sighting, I felt like I was being followed. On one occasion, I felt I was being watched by an unidentified 'creature' that appeared to be standing on its hind legs and appeared to be much larger than a human being. It was standing in a clearing, no trees around but the distance prevented a clear visualization of it. Since the initial sighting, I have been able to sense, without fail, when someone is watching or following me. At the initial sighting I was able to observe it for at least five minutes before it disappeared. I also noted at the time that the one light nearby on a hill went out. It was a clear evening, starry skies and warm, 85 degrees."

Stonewood Sighting
October 17, 1993
"Child's Top"
Karen S. Heaster

"Deciding to "shut down" for the night, I made the normal rounds of my home, the last being to look out the front door before locking up.

"Noticing a strange-looking light coming from the south, I made the brave decision to cross the street and watch it approach. As it moved closer to me, traveling south to east, I began to notice it take shape.

"The only way I know how to describe the shape was that of an old fashioned metal pump top. It is now southeast to me and moving at a moderate speed, slowly lowering its altitude. At about 15,000 feet, it made a straight path for the high hill opposite me.

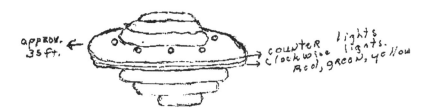

"The scream I heard was my own. I was sure that it was going to crash into the residences on the hill.

I would estimate it was approximately 35 feet in diameter.

"My neighbor ran onto his porch to see if someone had 'grabbed me,' and I was too spellbound to answer him. He came across the street to see if I needed help and saw it stop instantly, with two rows of lights in the center portion, one going clockwise and the other counterclockwise.

"These lights seemed to be the main control of its ability to stop instantly and leave just as quickly.

"This is what happened...it raised slightly on its side, went over the top of the hill out of sight.

"The severe headache I experienced that night and the next day could have been from 1. the object, 2. my excitement, 3. the fact that the sighting took place at 1:10 a.m. and I had difficulty sleeping.

"I do know one thing, I will never forget what I saw or the feeling of doom for the people up on the hill here in Stonewood."

Dark, burnt silver color.

Jamie Currey
As told to Karen Heaster
April 14, 1994
9:30 - 10:00 pm

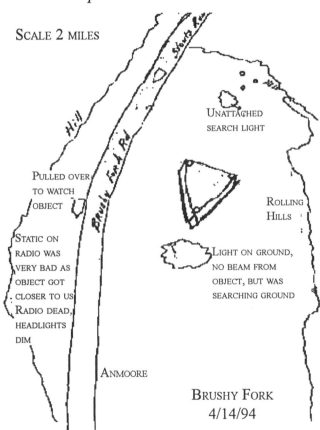

SCALE 2 MILES

UNATTACHED SEARCH LIGHT

PULLED OVER TO WATCH OBJECT

ROLLING HILLS

STATIC ON RADIO WAS VERY BAD AS OBJECT GOT CLOSER TO US. RADIO DEAD, HEADLIGHTS DIM

LIGHT ON GROUND, NO BEAM FROM OBJECT, BUT WAS SEARCHING GROUND

ANMOORE

BRUSHY FORK
4/14/94

"Jamie and her friend were out for a drive on Brushy Fork Road towards Stout's Run. On the way home, Jamie looked over her friend's shoulder and noticed three lights in a nearby field. She asked her friend to slow down. He noticed the lights and pulled over to the side of the road. They saw a white light searching the ground with no apparent beam attached to indicate its source. There were three lights in the sky, one red and two green. These three lights approached the vicinity of their car and they noticed the lights were on a triangular-shaped craft, approximately 15 to 18 feet wide. Static came over their radio and they turned it off. They noticed a red glow in the center of the craft. He tried to start the car and it was slow in starting.

The object then veered off to the south towards Anmore. They drove home."

"Karen reported that a friend who lives outside of Bridgeport, saw the same thing on the same night about 11:30 p.m."

Karen Heaster
August 13,
1994

Driving down Rt. 58, I noticed the object because the lights reflected on my car and arm, turning both green. I had no idea what the object was. It was awesome, very close—I hesitated at the intersection wanting to turn left to see where it went, but an eerie feeling made me turn right and go on to my mother-in-law's home. The object swooped over my car at about 300 feet. It went over the hill and from the green reflection, I thought it landed. I lost sight of it when it went over the hill and after a few seconds, reflection of green disappeared.

Dave described seeing much the same thing.

Same object was seen by Debra and (name) Hayhurst on Rt. 58 at Anmore at 12:20 a.m. on August 14. This time it was traveling from east to northeast. Appeared to land or disappear behind hill between Stonewood and Anmoore.

October 10, 1993: Seventeen-year-old Heather Heaster, Karen's daughter, has also had her share of sightings. The high school junior writes: "At first I thought it was an airplane. Its pulsating lights made me notice it. The amber lights and the outline were visible with the naked eye. With binoculars, I could see that the amber lights looked like large spotlights. It kept moving very slowly and ascending, until it disappeared over the horizon.

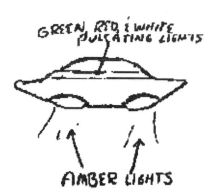

From Mufon Report:

October 18, 1993
Deborah L. Hayhurst
Stonewood, WV

I was in my front yard watching the sky at the request of my neighbor in order to help identify a light in the NW sky. I knew it was not a plane, but did not realize what it was. I was very excited when it got closer, but I was afraid at the same time. The strange shape hovered, then started doing figure 8's and fast maneuvers as if to show off, then it just disappeared over the hill in the west.

Thanks for the Help!

I wish to gratefully acknowledge the help of the following people in compiling the material for this chapter: MUFON Assistant State Director, Gregg Knight, Field Investigator, Karen Heaster, and all of those who granted permission to use their stories.

Karen Heaster. Photo by Bob Teets.

Chapter Fifteen

An Investigator's Initiation

These two stories deserve a chapter of their own for many reasons, but primarily because they reminded me of the old days when I was a newspaper reporter. They helped me remember lessons I had forgotten.

One of the prime reasons I drove 4 ½ hours to Beckley from my home was so I could meet the central character of the first story, "Mr. X," the name I had given him after he had refused to identify himself. He had told me on the phone that he would be willing to meet and to show me various important spots where his experience had taken place. We had arranged to meet at the mall where the story had allegedly begun a few years earlier.

He never showed.

He stiffed me on two other occasions, as well.

Just another day at the office.

Crossroads Mall
Beckley, WV 1992

Bull had just watched a late showing of *Batman* at the mall theatre, and was in his car pulling out of the parking lot, heading towards Beckley. It was around 3 a.m.

A short distance up the highway, he noticed a blonde-haired woman running alongside the road. As his headlights gradually illuminated her more, he could see that she was perhaps seven or eight months pregnant, and appeared to be frantic in her pace.

He pulled alongside her, rolled down the window and asked if he could help in any way. "Before I could get the words out of my mouth, she had jumped in the car, screaming, 'GET OUT OF HERE! THEY'RE AFTER ME!'"

Bull floored the '83 Mustang's accelerator—the car shot off in a roar.

Artist Susan Williams' sketch of a key scene from "Bull's" story.

A few seconds later and glancing in the rearview mirror, Bull noticed headlights swooping up behind his car. He was sure they belonged to a vehicle being commanded by an irate husband or boyfriend, probably drunk, and probably looking to pound on somebody.

"GO! GET OUT OF HERE!" the woman passenger screamed again, "THEY'RE RIGHT BEHIND US!"

Bull's heart pounded at his chest. "What have I got myself into?" he asked.

He gunned the Mustang through stoplights and stop signs, all the while with the woman screaming and the headlights behind him seemingly glued to his bumper.

"She was screaming the whole time," he said, "and I was rattled. She scared me to death—that and those headlights. What if that car back there had more than one person in it? And what if she had just stuffed a pillow under her shirt and was going to rob me? I didn't know what to think."

After passing through most of the town at breakneck speed, Bull felt a little easier when they entered a four-lane stretch of highway that would lead them to the Interstate, where he figured he could outrun anything or maybe find some help. Just as he let the Mustang have its head, the woman shrieked—"TURN HERE!"

Reflexively, Bull slammed the 'Stang into third, hit the brakes, skidded sideways and somehow negotiated the car onto the side road she had indicated. He punched the throttle, hit fourth gear and whisked up over a hill.

—the lights once again appeared right behind him.

"Enough!" Bull yelled, and he slammed on the brakes—

—just as the lights behind him...*flew up over top of the Mustang and hung in midair only yards above them!*

"GET OUT OF HERE!" the woman screamed again, and again Bull tested the car's speed, this time in reverse.

He finally spun the Mustang around in the road and shot back toward Beckley.

"No matter where I went," he said, "the lights stayed with me. It knew where I was going, 'cause it turned when I did, it went over a bridge when I went under it."

Just then, the woman screeched, "TURN HERE! IT'S MY GRANDFATHER'S HOUSE!"

Bull skidded into the driveway—the woman jumped out, ran across the yard and disappeared into the old, decrepit house—just as the lights from behind once again flew up over the Mustang, hovered a second or two, then shot off into the night in the wink of an eye.

Bull fled.

Many things now stand out in Bull's mind as he recalls that night.

When he got home, he says, the clock in the Mustang and the clocks in the house registered a three-minute difference. Bull says he's a stickler for maintaining the correct times on all his clocks, and regularly checks them according to the time that registers on his satellite dish. His car lights and fog lights constantly blow bulbs now, and never had before, he adds.

Those are inconsequential when compared to what he recalls about the female.

First of all, the woman—who Bull described as being "real pretty, with a petite face not swollen like a normal pregnant woman's face is"—was wearing a bright green blouse, but somehow it seemed to absorb rather than to reflect light. Secondly, Bull noticed that the slacks she was wearing as she sat in the passenger seat had not one wrinkle or crease in them, not even at the points where her body curved, like at the hips or knees. "It was like the material in the slacks was a solid of some sort," he says, "or a liquid."

A few weeks after the incident and on his return to Beckley, Bull says, he retraced the route they had taken that night, and eventually ended up at the old house the woman had said belonged to her grandfather. In the daylight, he says, "the place looked abandoned, it looked like nobody could have lived in it because of its condition."

He's suffered many cold sweats since that incident, he claims.

THE SECRET PAPERS

"I want some money to start my life over again," the caller said when I came on the line. It was a strange-sounding voice, with a hint of an accent. A foreigner of some sort, I thought. He was at a pay phone somewhere, because I could hear street noise in the background. "I have some information about the national space cover-up."

"What sort of information?" I asked.

"I have national security clearance, and I'm prepared to release certain information."

"What sort of information?" I repeated.

The nervous voice started talking about his having worked at a secret facility where he one day came across *several hundred pounds* of documents that had been destined for the shredder, but which he had somehow sidetracked into his possession. These documents allegedly outlined various covert projects being carried out by the government and involving UFOs and such.

Further, he said he had seen the original MJ-12 papers, alien bodies at a facility in Texas, and that the project he and 350 others had been working on involved human teleportation and other things. The project was under round-the-clock protection of armed soldiers who carried laser-sighted rifles. He said he has written a book about all of it, but that he wanted to sell everything to me.

He said he had neglected many of the original documents and had subsequently lost them, and that now, "government agents" were making his life a living hell.

"The public deserves to know the truth," he said.

"This is my initiation," I thought. I had read of the "Men In Black" who had harassed UFO percipients and researchers alike. I had followed accounts of other researchers who had been taken in by mysterious persons who claimed to be military insiders or "special ops" agents suddenly overcome by bouts of guilt or other motivations and who wanted to come clean. Secret films, tapes, photos, documents and other materials were all offered as proof of their claims.

And yet, they all turned out to be ruses, aimed at discrediting researchers or percipients.

Now, it was my turn.

"Why me?" I asked the mystery man. "I'm nobody. I live in the boondocks of West Virginia. Why didn't you contact some big-time names, the ones who write all the books, have all the resources?"

"I saw you on television," he answered, "and you looked like a nice guy, somebody I could trust."

Whoa, had that been a play for my ego (even though, of course, he had been correct!)?

"I do my research in the public domain," I said. "No secret stuff. And nothing illegal. You should take your materials to one of the big names."

"The public has a right to know," he said nervously.

"I couldn't agree more," I replied.

"I-I'm not asking for much," he said, "thirty, maybe forty-thousand at the most. I need to start over, me and my family."

I truly felt sorry for him at that point. If he was telling the truth, he deserved pity, for the consequences of his actions would probably lead to disaster for him and his family...and even, potentially, for America.

I was really stumped.

He ended the conversation by telling me I could send my decision in a letter addressed to a post office box number in a certain town.

Later, I wrote a letter that outlined why I thought I couldn't participate in his plans unless he could assure me that he was not involved in anything illegal, or that his actions would not confront my own sense of ethics. I also explained that I didn't have financial resources available to me that would meet his expectations, though I didn't consider them large.

I hope I didn't make a mistake. Not because of missing the potentially biggest story of all time. But because I worried that if he was telling the truth, his life may well have been in danger.

I haven't heard from him since.

I worry about him now.

A rough initiation...for both of us.

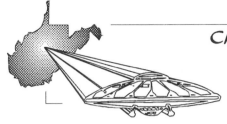

Chapter Sixteen

Harvest Time
In Elk Garden

The small town of Elk Garden, population approximately 300, is on the fringe of what famous UFO researcher and Mountain State native Gray Barker called the "Mini Bermuda Triangle" of the United States: Preston, Taylor and Tucker Counties, West Virginia. Though not within the boundaries of these three counties, Elk Garden, located in Mineral County, is close enough to qualify, should it wish such a distinction.

Situated on a hilly plateau atop the rugged and coal-rich mountains straddling the Maryland-West Virginia border and a few thousand feet above the picturesque Potomac River, the town and its surroundings bespeak the glory days of a rollicking King Coal/land baron aristocracy.

A large, level area of town devoid of buildings is said to have been reserved for the courthouse and other public buildings anticipated to be built at the time when the town's economy and political muscle were thought to be sufficient enough to consolidate power into this area of the county.

The view of the western horizon above Elk Garden reveals mountains of coal, a staple of the small town's economy. The arm of a large coal shovel is barely visible in the top center of the photo. Photo by Bob Teets.

Ramshackle, boarded up storefronts now tell of the failed effort to do so, as the boom and bust cycle so prevalent in a coal economy pulled the rug from beneath the grandiose scheme.

Now, however, the local economy is showing promise as, once again, the coal business seems literally on an upward trend, at least when you look on the horizon above town. Where deep mines once plunged into the hillsides, giant shovels and earth-moving equipment now dig, scratch and claw at various open-air strip mine sites around and on top of the hills.

Just a few hundred yards south of a busy strip mine visible from town is a place called Nethken Hill.

The scene here is the type Norman Rockwell would have painted should he have sought to depict a reverential shrine of old-fashioned America. Slightly windward of the hill and amid the shade of pine and maple trees is a beautiful little church, the Nethken Hill Methodist, constructed in 1875 to replace an older structure on land donated years before by the Nethken family, coal mine operators at the time.

The church is surrounded by cemeteries with gravestones dating into the early part of the last century. The cemetery on the right, or northern side, of the church contains numerous markers denoting the burial sites of many Nethkens and other prominent names of the area. On the southern side of the church is the so-called "Kalbaugh" graveyard. Across the lane, to

The Nethken Hill Methodist Church, built shortly after the Civil War to replace an older structure, has been the gathering spot for generations of Elk Garden faithful. The Dean family memorial is in the foreground at left.

the east, is the much larger R. D. Dean Memorial I.O.O.F. (International Order of Odd Fellows) cemetery. A gravestone here resembling a small replica of the Washington Monument rises above the Dean family burial plot.

At first, there is no sound here but that of the shutter release on my camera. Soon, however, the unmistakable rumble and roar of mining equip-

The entrance to the R. D. Dean Memorial I.O.O.F. cemetery. Note the Nethken Hill Methodist Church to the right of center in the background.

ment starting up over at the mine site adds a sort of tribute to those whose remains were buried here after they had finished their toils in the now silent mines which they excavated deeper still beneath this and surrounding hills.

Visiting in late September, at a time when farmers are gathering in their crops for storage in sometimes quaint, sometimes modern barns, and when sawmill operators are hauling loads of hardwood timber along narrow country lanes, and while strip miners are extracting their precious ore, one marvels at the bounty of Elk Garden and the miles of undulating hills around it, a place which has sustained generations of families, and which was recognized for its riches long before the arrival of the white man. Sitting on a hill overlooking the quiet, sunlit valleys, you can almost hear the near silent footfalls of the American Indians who long ago followed well-worn trails into these mountains in search of the vast herds of elk and other wildlife that flourished here.

Indeed, on this late summer day, it is as if Elk Garden were the Garden of Eden, a place of bounty and never-ending harvest.

There was a time, though, when the Garden wasn't so bucolic.

CURIOUS VISITORS?

Though resident Gene M. Smith reported having seen UFOs as early as 1964 in the Elk Garden area, it wasn't until the latter part of the decade that extraordinary events occurred throughout the area, but particularly in the vicinity of Nethken Hill.

The Jones family, prominent farmers in the area, recalled a hair-raising experience.

It was sometime in April, 1968. Presidential candidate Robert F. Kennedy was two months away from assassin Sirhan Bishara Sirhan's fatal attack in a Los Angeles, California, hotel, while the Rev. Martin Luther King had only recently fallen to the deadly aim of escaped convict James Earl Ray. It was the beginning of America's "long hot summer," as civil unrest fanned shouts of "Burn, baby, burn!" amidst cities on fire.

Emmett and Pauline Jones wondered if the flames were visible from high above the earth, and if such fires had perhaps brought curious visitors to earth, and later to their 2,000-acre farm one night.

It all started when the Jones' son, Wayne, and his eight-month pregnant wife, Brenda, couldn't sleep. They decided they may as well check the livestock, which at that time included upwards of a hundred head of cattle and other animals.

Storm clouds from earlier in the day had given way to a crystal clear night that one can only experience in the mountains.

They climbed into their 1962 Oldsmobile and drove a short distance on Route 42 through Elk Garden, which their farm partially surrounds, then began checking the fence row as they exited town, headed south.

Just then, Brenda noticed something up in the direction of Nethken Hill. "What's that light?" she asked Wayne.

He stopped the car and stepped out, thinking at first that it must be a helicopter. Curious though, it seemed to have come from out of the ground.

The light seemed to be approaching their car.

All at once, he could see that it was more than one light, and that the one in front seemed to be moving even more boldly toward him.

Suddenly, it was right over top of him, a huge, 100-foot round orange light that glowed "bright enough you wouldn't have needed headlights," Wayne remembered. Because the light was so bright, he couldn't make out a shape other than that it was perfectly round, but he could see two torpedo-shaped tanks of some kind fastened to the bottom. The only sound coming from the massive object reminded Wayne of a relatively quiet refrigerator motor.

It scared both Wayne and Brenda, so he hopped back in the car, turned it around and dashed back into town at 50 or 60 m.p.h.—

—the light remaining overhead.

By the time the Oldsmobile pulled into Emmett and Pauline's driveway, the light had stopped following them, and had instead remained hovering over a spot a short distance away.

But only temporarily.

"We got Mom and Dad out of bed and told them what we'd seen," Wayne recalled. "They came outside and they couldn't believe it, you know."

The light moved slowly west, then hovered unsteadily no more than 10 to 15 degrees above the silo next to the family's barn, its light so bright that the silo shone like silver.

"It gave us a funny feeling," Pauline said, "so we turned off all the lights in the house."

At various times, the object would sprout flames for 10 to 12 seconds around its perimeter, "like when you light up a gas stove," Wayne explained.

It would move from one place to another in rapid order. "When it moved, it moved fast," Emmett said.

The family stood in awe and watched the object and others like it in the distance for perhaps 30 minutes. It wasn't until the objects started moving off toward the west that Wayne and Emmett got a rifle from inside the house and watched the object through the rifle's scope.

Sometime later, a military man, perhaps Air Force, from Washington, DC paid Wayne a visit and asked to hear his story, particularly about the

sounds associated with the sighting. Later, Wayne said, the man told him that he thought the Jones family had witnessed the aurora borealis.

"What we saw wasn't the northern lights," Wayne told me. "I know what I saw." He said it scared Brenda so bad that they feared she may go into early labor, or worse.

And then, on May 3, 1968, their daughter Sheri was born. "She had a birthmark," Wayne explained, "right behind her right ear. It was a perfect circle, and it was orange, just like that light. She still has it, though it's not as visible now."

THE LIGHTS OF NETHKEN HILL

"We'd see lights all during the late 1960's and early '70's going back and forth around the church area," Amie Kalbaugh, 39, said. "I never wanted to see them, but I did."

The Kalbaugh residence is located on a 100-acre farm on the western side of Nethken Hill, down a hollow and only a few hundred yards away from the Methodist Church and its surrounding cemeteries.

"We would watch the lights and go through a process of elimination, 'not a plane, not a helicopter,' and so forth, and try to figure out what they were," Amie, who was a teenager at the time, said. "I always thought we heard a high-pitched sound and then we would look out the window. The lights were always white."

She recalled one specific time in which her older sister, Vickie, tried to get her to come to the window and watch a "mother ship" hover over the meadow while smaller lights flew into it.

"It's hard to remember," Vickie, now a 41-year-old English teacher told me. "I do not have a very good memory. After these sightings, we were always so afraid."

She recalled one time, when she was a sophomore in high school, that, "I was down at a neighbor's pond, and I saw a silvery white, elliptical-shaped thing in the sky. I was thinking, 'That's not an airplane or a helicopter.' Your mind plays tricks on you when you're frightened, and I remember being afraid."

She said one other time she remembered hearing the cows lowing and the dogs barking, but that's all. "I don't want to remember, so I don't remember," she stated.

One other person besides Amie and Vickie in the Kalbaugh household recalled another sighting.

Clark Sharpless, who is director of transportation for the Garrett County, Maryland school district, was 25 at the time and married to one of the Kalbaugh girls.

It was very early on the morning of July 15 or 16, 1970, a day or two after the couples' daughter had been born, and they were staying at the Kalbaugh home.

"I can't remember why I was up," Clark said, "but I was looking out the window toward Nethken Hill Cemetery when I saw an object moving in the sky over the cemetery. I called for my wife to come to the window to look, but she was too sick, she'd just delivered our daughter—

"Within a flash, it's right over the house!

"I'm looking directly up at the bottom of this object which is possibly cigar-shaped to elliptical, somewhere in between. A lot of bright lights on the bottom, very bright. Ten to 15 bright lights. As quickly as it's there— *Bam*! It's gone again. Then I see the lights again toward Elk Garden, on Nethken Hill Cemetery again.

"I observed this for maybe 30 minutes. Off and on it would be various places, but it would move very quickly. Lights would move within a snap of your fingers.

A sketch of the craft Clark Sharpless saw in mid-July, 1970 while staying at the Kalbaugh residence near the Nethken Hill Methodist Church. Drawn in 1994 by Clark.

Clark said he did not go outside. "I was ill at ease to say the least," he added. "I really wasn't fearful. I didn't feel I was in any danger, but I was excited! I remember I tore the blind down off the window in my excitement."

I asked him if he thought it was intelligently driven.

"Yes. Certainly, it was very sophisticated to have that kind of movement. Assuming it was the same craft, over there and overhead, you could not see the movement, it was *zip! zip!*— here and gone."

He did not believe it to be any type of conventional aircraft, and it had no sound.

(One curious aspect of this story is that Clark said the government later contacted him and had him fill out a report form. As UFO researchers know, however, *Project Blue Book*, the official U.S. Air Force investigation into UFOs, was announced as officially ending in 1969, a year before Clark was contacted. So, what government agency contacted him?)

Another member of the Kalbaugh family, Gary, who is now 49, "...never did see anything that I would describe as a UFO while living there."

The Keyser Middle School science teacher said he and a bus load of

The Scene Of A Mystery:

A two-photo splice of the panoramic view of the Nethken Hill Methodist Church and cemeteries, above, and the Kalbaugh residence, with only the roof visible, down over the embankment at right.

students returning from a field trip one time did see something unusual, but that he couldn't recall details.

His reaction to stories about sightings on Nethken Hill?

"I know most of these people, and my sisters wouldn't try to mislead anyone," he answered. "It would have been interesting to have seen one. I'm open, I think that there could be something like UFOs."

Mrs. Kalbaugh, the mother, told me she had never seen a UFO, either.

UFOs On Nethken Hill

It was from the left of the perspective of this photo that Rev. Harley DeLuerere and two other men watched events unfold on the night of October 8, 1967, just hours after a funeral.

Her sister, Mrs. Zona Dixon, said she once saw some unusual lights repeatedly going straight up, then straight down over a distant hill. The next morning, some boys who lived in the vicinity of the hill told her at school, "'Oh, Mrs. Dixon, you should have seen what we saw last night!' They said they saw UFOs that had come down, and one was long like a cigar. There were different shapes, and there were about five of them, they said."

A lot of people in Elk Garden remember the period when plenty of rumors about strange lights and flying objects would result in sometimes carloads of people driving up to the church for a nighttime vigil.

I talked with several residents who said they had spent many nights on Nethken Hill watching for UFOs and had never seen anything unusual. One such man, William Michaels, 64, said, "I went up there lots of times, and I never saw a thing."

William was the grave digger for the cemeteries at the time. He said he would dig the graves during the nighttime hours, because it was cooler.

I met Howard Dawson, 77, a retired coal miner, while I was photographing the Nethken Hill area. "I came up here, sat in the car, got out and walked around," he said. "I've never seen any UFOs up here."

I spoke with David M. McIntyre, who used to work for Brown's Television company in Cresaptown, Maryland, and who repeatedly accompanied his boss and others to Elk Garden, sometimes in the company airplane, looking for UFOs or signs of them. Though they never saw anything, David did speak with many of the eyewitnesses back then. "Those people up there saw something," he said. "There are too many of them who have seen something for them to be making this up."

One who did see something was 53-year-old Dixon Ridder, a local mail carrier and sort of unofficial local historian. He remembered two sightings.

Born a few miles away in Kitzmiller, Maryland, his roots stretch back six generations in this

Dixon Ridder. Photo by Bob Teets.

area. He now lives about a mile north of Nethken Hill.

It had been his phone call to me on July 20, 1994, which had led me to Elk Garden a few months later. During the afternoon of my visit, he acted as a guide while we traveled the area in his pickup.

We eventually ended up walking out across the hillside that overlooks the Nethken Hill church and the Kalbaugh residence.

"I saw a brilliant white light with a sharp outline of its edge right over there," he said, pointing to the rear of the church. "It was about five feet in diameter, and was just a few feet back from the church. It lit up the whole area. All of a sudden, it went to the back of the church, then went across the road to that Dean Monument over there, where, just like you turn a light out, it vanished."

(One sighting reported by a Hopi Indian woman in 1970 mentioned that a UFO looked like a moon, and that after performing some aerial feats, it "turned off its light like a light bulb."[1] Other accounts in this book rely on the same imagery, see Larry Gibson's story on Page 20.)

The entire incident lasted only a few seconds, as the light had moved quickly from place to place.

He saw another light on a different occasion, this time while riding his motorcycle late one night. "I came up over the hill and there was a yellow light, small yellow light moving around a little bit. I thought, well, maybe it was a light from a window of a house down over the hill. But the more I watched it, the more it carried on."

He had a few minutes earlier passed his cousin and a girlfriend, so he doubled back and got them.

"They drove up, she and I walked down toward the light. It appeared again and danced around and everything. The next day I was up on the hill...and I couldn't see the house, so I knew it wasn't a light from there."

Dixon admitted good-naturedly to having one night sped along the road past the church on his motorcycle while a girlfriend held an old, lighted lantern aloft on the end of a pitchfork when a pickup load of men were watching near the church. One other time, he and another motorist across from him saw each other's headlights. Later, "We got to laughing because we both thought we were seeing flying saucers," he said.

Perhaps the funniest incident he recalled was that of a man who one

1. *American Indian Myths & Mysteries*; Gaddis, Vincent H.; Indian Head Books, New York

night decided to take a shortcut to his home by walking through the cemetery. Suddenly, something "grabbed ahold of him, and he took off running and yelling." The man fought the tenacious specter until he arrived home and discovered that it had been a length of prickly briar which had caught on his pants.

A Trio Observes the Nethken Hill Lights

It was no ruse witnessed one night by a trio of men.

It was late on Sunday evening, October 8, 1967.

Reverend Harley DeLeurere, a circuit-riding Methodist minister who was two days away from his 27th birthday, answered the knock on his door, and greeted the town's mayor, Leonard P., and his 32-year-old son, Leonard Jr. (*Note: the latter two mens' names have been changed.*)

"Come with us," the older man said, "We're going to Nethken Hill."

Without hesitation, Harley agreed. He, like the two men of his church congregation he was accompanying to the hill, had heard the stories circulating around town about strange lights up on the hill. Everyone was curious.

Besides, there had been a funeral earlier in the day.[2]

And so, the trio proceeded to a spot about a quarter-mile northwest of the Nethken Hill Methodist Church where Harley preached every other Sunday morning. From this vantage point, they had a commanding view of the church and cemeteries on their left, and of a narrow hollow which led a few hundred yards down to their right, where the Kalbaugh family residence was located.

For two hours they sat and talked...and waited.

Suddenly, they saw a flash of light in the sky.

Lightning?

No, there was a clear sky.

Headlights coming up over the hill?

No, there was no traffic this late at night.

Airplane lights?

No air traffic, either.

They discussed the possibilities, but couldn't come up with a reasonable answer.

---

2. Ms. Amy Sharpless, who was an undertaker at the time, confirmed that a funeral had taken place in the I.O.O.F. cemetery on October 8, 1967.

Artist Susan Williams' interpretation of the Nethken Hill sighting by Rev. Harley DeLeurere and two other Elk Garden men on October 8, 1967.

Then—

"Look," one of them said, pointing toward the Kalbaugh house.

The three watched in awe as what Leonard Jr. later described as "something like a big turtle with lights on it appeared level with the top of the house" and then moved purposely up the hollow toward the church.

"It was like two headlights floating along," Harley said later, "that left an erratic trail, like you see in a time exposure photograph."

Soon, "It wasn't more than six feet off the ground," Leonard Jr. said, "and it had three or four recessed lights on it that shined toward the graveyard and down on the ground, too."

The two mens' memories diverge at this point (Leonard, Sr. having died many years ago), though they nonetheless agree that the object flew over, first the Nethken Hill Methodist Church cemetery, then over the I.O.O.F. cemetery.

Leonard Jr. remembers the object momentarily hovering and shinning its lights down onto a day-old grave in the I.O.O.F. cemetery. Rev. DeLeurere does not recall that detail. Leonard Jr. said he recalled the minister suggesting later that the casket in the new grave should be exhumed and the body checked for signs of any disturbance. Rev. Harley does not recall that detail, though he said he may have made such a remark in passing.

Both say that when the lights disappeared, they, being younger than Leonard Sr., ran from their position for a closer look, but upon arriving at the cemeteries, there was nothing to be seen. "We thought sure we'd see something," Leonard Jr. said, "but when we got there, there wasn't anything."

The lights, both men said, had simply disappeared.

Leonard Jr. had seen other objects both before and after this sighting, in other parts of the area. One sighting occurred as he was delivering milk from his farm about five miles away, out on Route 50. It was daylight that time, and Leonard said two other motorists pulled up alongside his pickup and watched three discs surrounded by "a greenish, yellow haze" hover in the eastern sky until "one left so fast you couldn't see it, and the other two followed just as fast." On another occasion, he said, "I would see them while I was cutting hay up in the field." These sightings occurred years apart, he added.

But the most intriguing sighting remained to be the one on Nethken Hill, he said. "It seemed like every time there was a new grave, within the next couple of nights, people would see lights up there."

Chapter Seventeen

Think Of All
The Possibilities

A 1970's children's television program entitled "Make a Wish" used as its theme an admonition to its viewers to open their minds and to, "Think of all the possibilities."

The Elk Garden/Nethken Hill case (and many others contained in this book) challenges us to do the same.

What, in fact, did happen in that small, rural community so many years ago?

While it would take many more books than this one to adequately address that question, here's a brief overview of possibilities:

* It is possible that one or more people perpetrated a lengthy, certainly expensive and technologically sophisticated three- or four-year-long hoax that fooled a lot of people.

Apparently, they or a copycat hoaxer decided, after a long respite, to renew the trick, as Amie Kalbaugh reported once again seeing a slow-moving, soccer ball-sized globe of light in the late 1980's— nearly twenty years after the last reported sighting in the area. The globe, she said, was moving no more than 15 to 20 feet over her head and slow enough that she could have kept up with it at a jogging pace. Instead, however, she ran to the house.

* Given the Jones family reports and descriptions, there is a chance that their sighting was of a secret aircraft under development by our or another government. Recall in the 1952 case of the Flatwoods Green Monster (see Page 11) that Kathleen May Horner claimed a reporter read to her a letter from "the government" which said the "green monster" was, in fact, a prototype of a missile under development to reach the moon.

The mystery still remains, however, that mention was made of "pilots" who were somehow flying along with the missiles in either launch vehicles or in "shadow planes" to monitor the missiles. One such vehicle supposedly either crashed or landed nearby and left "skid marks" down over a hill near where the green monster/missile was spotted. If this were true, then whatever became of the pilots?

Further, as Ivan Sanderson noted, there were at least two additional crashes of "constructions" in the general vicinity. Did these missiles similarly have pilots aboard? If so, what were their fates? It sure does appear as if further research is called for, because either way—"monster" or ultra-sophisticated (for the time) technology—the Flatwoods case may, in fact, be more important than the now disputed Roswell, New Mexico incident of 1947. Combined with the Elk Garden / Nethken Hill Case, the possibilities are most intriguing.

* No one to this point would rule out the possibility that these anomalous phenomena could be explained in more prosaic terms, like naturally occurring ball lighting or northern lights, low-flying weather balloons, tectonic stress or anomalous electromagnetic lights, or as a hundred other sometimes theoretical but nonetheless potentially observable scientific items of interest.

But what if none of those possibilities is on the mark? What then?

Well, tighten that seat belt, 'cause we're about to take a sharp turn into the unknown. We have no map, and our only guide is the *Matrix of UFO Beliefs* (see Appendix A), and the unofficial taxonomy on Page 17.

Since it is not my intent to present an epistemological examination of the phenomenon here, I'll stick to *highlighting* an area I find the most fascinating in connection with UFOs: the religious / spiritual aspects. While others may argue differently, I see these issues as most central to an examination of the phenomenon.

SEARCH FOR INTENT VIA ITS EFFECTS

The debate, of course, is still open about the existence of UFOs, and whether there are living entities associated with them. For the moment, let's assume that UFOs are real and that they are connected to living entities of some kind, if even incorporeal (at least to human detection) or mere "intelligence." That's where all of the following people start from.

As a whole, UFO beings, what or whoever they are, have only so many ways of interacting with us. Too, humans are prone to seeing and reacting in ways that they have learned from their cultural heritage and individual upbringing. This leads us to say that one person's demon may be another's angel may be another's alien may be another's "germ." Thus, we have only the *effects* of these contacts on people to help us ascertain the *intent* of the contacts.

The lines blur rapidly. Here are some examples and how they relate to the Elk Garden / Nethken Hill case and others mentioned in this book.

NATIVE AMERICAN INDIAN INFLUENCES

According to the book, *American Indian Myths and Mysteries*[1], the Hopi Indian tribe of the southwest U.S. is inexorably linked with the UFO phenomenon because its members believe many of their deities, the so-called *kachinas*, are from other planets. One chief is reported to have stated point blank, "We have seen the flying saucers and have heard their message to us... Also, Hopi Indians know that other planets and worlds have people, and they are watching us." The message alluded to by the chief is the belief that, if the Hopi people remain true to their old teachings and beliefs, they will be safely removed from earth and taken to another planet at the time of the "Great Purification." (Note also the connection of being a "chosen people" who will be "saved" so long as they adhere to their founding belief structure. This, of course, is akin to other religious and/or political belief structures throughout time. Christians may refer to a similar "Rapture" that will come in the "End Times.") The chief's remarks were believed to have been made in July, 1969, a time identical to that of many Elk Garden sightings.

It is noteworthy to mention here that the road leading between the cemeteries and past the Nethken Hill Methodist Church is, according to Dixon Ridder, an old Indian trail (though not a Hopi trail).

Other Amerindian beliefs suggest comparisons with the Elk Garden / Nethken Hill episodes, as well.

In *People of the Web*[2], author Gregory L. Little says Indians believe that as humans became more and more technologically attuned, they began harming the earth in an effort to control it, and as a result began losing

1. *American Indian Myths and Mysteries*, by Vincent H. Gaddis, 1992, Indian Head Books, New York, New York.

2. *People of the Web*, by Gregory L. Little, White Buffalo Books, Memphis, Tennessee.

touch with the spirits around them. These spirits, demanding attention in order for humans to be complete and to assure kindness to the "earth mother," will stop at nothing to regain humans' notice, and that many times, they will present themselves in a corporeal form acceptable to humans' cultural and technological belief system at the time.

It is true that hundreds of UFO contactees report, after their experience with UFOs, a renewed interest in earth ecology and in their own spirituality. By the same token there are contactees who are inalterably traumatized, or at least changed in a negative way, by their experiences, to be discussed in more detail later.

One possibility for the Elk Garden sightings, then, could be linked to the earth spirits recognized by Amerindians, presumably even those who once traveled on a trail that would become a road past the Nethken Hill Methodist Church and where strip mines and deep mines once harmed the earth mother. It could be argued, then, that more modern mining methods instituted and legislated in the 1970's and '80's have proven acceptable to the earth spirits in and around Elk Garden and thus accounts for the reason why the "spirits" haven't been sighted since that time.

TWO BRIEF POSSIBILITIES

Briefly, two other possibilities with broader applications include:

* War historian William Bramley (author of *The Gods of Eden*) discovered what he calls "Custodians," which he believes are the root cause of human warfare and divisiveness. Bramley certainly links the Custodians with UFOs, seeing them as basically malevolent entities who control us, essentially, for fun and profit.[3]

* Vladimir Terziski, a Bulgarian immigrant who now lectures at UFO conferences and runs the "American Academy of Dissident Sciences," a nonprofit organization, often refers to the phenomenon as a "management system," controlled by competing consorts of terrestrial opinion-makers and off-planet intelligences.[4]

---

3. *The Gods of Eden, by William Bramley, 1993, Avon Books, New York, New York.*

4. Statements made during the 1993 International MUFON Symposium in Richmond, Virginia, and elsewhere.

others consider central to interpreting the phenomenon.

"There can be little place, especially within the Judeo-Christian tradition for a variety of small, but powerful homely beings who administer an odd mixture of trauma and transcendence without apparent regard for any established religious hierarchy or doctrine," Mack, a Pulitzer prize-winning author, writes. "At best, this would seem puzzling and difficult to integrate. At worst, to the polarizing perception of Christian dualism these dark-eyed beings must seem to be the playmates of the Devil."

To offset the limiting possibilities of the "dualism" he sees, Dr. Mack, who also sits on the MUFON (Mutual UFO Network) board of directors, implies the need to supplant, or at least to broaden Christian doctrine with an openness to a newer crop of messengers, a techno-eco-spiritual fleet of beings who harbor good tidings for humans. Citing his synthesis of abductees' comments, he observes that these "...alien beings, although resented for their intrusive activities, may also be seen as intermediaries, closer than we are to God or the source of being."

One purpose of these messengers, he thinks, is to change human consciousness by breeding a superior race, part human, part alien.

"Abductions seem to be concerned primarily with two related projects: changing human consciousness to prevent the destruction of the earth's life, and a joining of two species for the creation of a new evolutionary form."

This dominant new, "hybrid breed" (also often referred to by abduction researchers Budd Hopkins, to whom Mack dedicates his book, and others) would presumably possess a gentler, kinder attitude toward the earth and not pollute it the way humans have. In the process, of course, the human race would loose its identity. Mack says, however, that the abductees he has studied seem powerless to stop the "hybrid" process.

The idea of changing human consciousness in order for the species to allow its own genetic code to be permanently altered comes not without some trauma, he says.

In concert with observations made by colleague Stanislav Grof, an M.D. psychiatrist who helped pioneer LSD-inspired research into nonordinary states of mind, and who co-developed (with Christina Grof) the drug-free "Holotropic Breath" modality of transformative psychology (which Dr. Mack acknowledges as having greatly influenced his consciousness and which he employs in his hypnotic work with abductees), Mack says that abductees generally pass through an "ego death" before they can achieve a breakthrough to higher consciousness and spiritual transformation wrought by the abduction experience.

Mack believes, in fact, that humankind as a whole may need to suffer a "cultural ego death" in order for us to experience an "evolution of consciousness."

Nonetheless, and while the aliens pursue their objectives, he says, there evolves a supplicating "love" between the alien captors and their human subjects.

To modulate such potentially consciousness-shattering findings, Mack adds a caveat mid-way in his summarizing final chapter: "It needs to be stressed that we do not know if any of the above phenomena exist literally on the purely material plane of reality... It could all be 'educational,' a kind of mythic drama, intended by a transcendent intelligence to move our being to a higher level. Or the merger of the alien and human species might be more literally real, its very awkwardness the result of the prodigious difficulty of bringing together a densely embodied race such as ours with more nearly spiritual entities like the alien beings."

Howls of Protest

Such a startling viewpoint, even with Mack's oddly placed caveat, has brought howls of protest from practically every quarter, except perhaps, from within the UFO "community," and interestingly, except from mainstream Judeo-Christian clergy or leadership.

Washington Post book reviewer Rudy Rucker wrote, "Why is it, finally, that I find *Abduction* so annoying? I guess it's because I love the idea of UFOs, and *Abduction* drags this idea into the mud."[10]

Newsweek[11] reviewers Peter Plagens and Martha Brant observed, "The aliens' green politics are... remarkably similar to Mack's; their agenda is to make a race that will stop polluting planet Earth... If we ever do accept the existence of alien body snatchers, it will be in spite of Mack's book, not because of it."

The *Atlantic Monthly*[12] published its own wry opinion that, "The book certainly offers the enticing possibility of debate unencumbered by fact."

---

10. *Washington Post* "Book World," Volume XXIV, Number 16

11. Newsweek, April 11, 1994

12. *Atlantic Monthly*, (date) 1994

A *Psychology Today*[13] article quoted University of California, Berkeley, social psychologist Richard Ofshe, also a Pulitzer Prize winner: "If there's a certain brilliance in backing the trendiest wrong horses available, then John Mack has it. He has made a stellar, absolutely impressive, world-class series of mistakes."

Time[14] magazine later ran another Ofshe observation: "If this were just an example of some zany new outer limit of how foolish psychology and psychiatry can be in the wrong hands, we'd look at it, roll our eyes and walk away. But the use of his (Mack's) techniques in counseling is substantially harming lots of people."

The same *Time* article also outlined disappointments voiced by former Mack research subjects, including one man who said, "He (Mack) was against anybody who said anything negative about the aliens."

Equally damning in the article was the revelation that, "...one of Mack's 'experiencers' has revealed to *Time* that she was actually an undercover debunker..." The debunker, Donna Bassett, alleged Mack's work was "riddled with scientific irregularities" and other deficiencies. She reportedly will include her findings in an upcoming book.

It is said Mack countered that he was sure Bassett was an abductee, and that her actions as a debunker were a mere extension of her desire to deny her abduction experiences.

Mack Calls for Colleagues' Help

The Harvard psychiatrist says his findings indicate that many of his more tradition-bound colleagues fail to help abductees when the practitioners employ rigid modalities, and he calls on them to beef up their knowledge of the phenomenon, if even not believing in it.

This seems a fair and logical request, even though the abduction experience and the psychology accompanying it seems to offer opportunities for interpretations far afield from Dr. Mack's.

If the UFO abduction experience is to be thoroughly examined within the field of psychology, it would certainly seem logical to suggest a far more broad and diverse group of investigators than are currently represented in most UFO research organizations. Dr. Baldwin, for example, would be an excellent addition to any such investigation.

13. *Psychology Today*, "The Harvard Professor and the UFOs," by Jill Niemark, March/April, 1994

14. *Time*, "The Man From Outer Space," April 18, 1994

A Personal Take on the Mack Thesis

Dr. Mack may, of course, be right in his assessment of what his abductee clients are saying.

Perhaps aliens are conducting a "soft invasion" in order to save us from ourselves. Maybe human destiny, having previously been altered by unexplainable events and "missing links" as a way of preserving it, is once again poised for a sea-change in its genetic makeup that will result in a less aggressive, less polluting, more "happy" creature.

Perhaps he is correct, as well, in saying that the abduction scenario is not evil, and that humankind may be facing an alternative reality which could result in all of these things coming true if we don't change our ways and heed the message given percipients.

It could be, as Dr. Mack suggests, that the Christian dualism he discounts is to be relegated to the past along with other remnants of the old human race.

The new dualism he observes may be the order of the day: By asserting that many *traumatic events* suffered by abductees as they traverse their paths to "higher consciousness" are *beneficial* in the long term, particularly when it comes to their new-found mission to help clean up the planet from pollution, Dr. Mack may be implying the abduction scenario as a sort of initiation into an eco-spiritual movement which many observers see as an emerging new religion. If so, it is a religion which demands the ultimate sacrifice—the "ethnic cleansing" or elimination of the abductees' entire species.

If such comes to pass, it will surely be humanity's last religious exercise.

Another Possibility

It may be that Dr. Baldwin has a better grasp of the situation.

Perhaps the invasion was foretold in the Bible with the expulsion of Lucifer and a third of the heavenly hosts that were cast to earth by the Archangel Michael.

In view of this, and until we as a species have been hybridized out of existence, it may well be time to once again review some doctrines that have served to aid humankind in other troubled times. Perhaps the invasion is real, and maybe the insurgents are gifted in many ways, but so far, they haven't won.

A political dissident once explained to me how he and millions of others helped to bring the awesome power of communism—once thought to be indestructible— to its knees. "Don't use guns," he said, "they have more and bigger guns. Their technology surpasses anything you have, too. There's an easier way. You put a grain of sand into the system's machinery every day—it eventually grinds to a halt."

The likely "grain of sand" to use in the case of "alien invaders," if that's what they are, is what UFO author George C. Andrews calls, "focusing the mind on powerful imagery, different for each individual." My interpretation of that statement means, "prayer."

---

15. *Extra-Terrestrial Friends and Foes*, by George C. Andrews, IllumiNet Press, Lilburn, Georgia

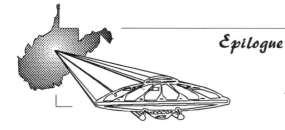

A Message
For Vern

Are we, like some suggest, targets for alien "soul snatchers"? Were the incidents witnessed on Nethken Hill the ultimate "abduction" experience, where departing souls were interrupted in their journey?

Or, were the sightings very special and limited "audience participation" episodes, where a handful of people actually got to see the ascension of souls or the angelic lights accompanying them?

Or, could these various lights merely have been curious visitors?

Or, could these entities have been messengers carrying a note to the eyewitnesses as a way of helping them seek "spiritual transformation"?

The questions never stop. And the answers seldom come.

For sure, the phenomenon and our reaction to it should not be about fear, because fear is paralyzing and self-destructive. If we are targets, then fear only adds to our vulnerability, because it's apparent that whatever is happening is at least partially or perhaps wholly dependent on us for its power.

Another way of saying it comes from two people featured in this book.

Nancy Workman (see her story on Page 136) said, "If you (UFOs) are alive, God created you, so I'm not afraid."

Clark Sharpless, who witnessed a spectacular event while staying at the Kalbaugh residence near Nethken Hill, said after nearly 25 years to reflect on it: "I did not necessarily have a spiritual awakening or anything, but I had thoughts of what Being might have made all of us and whoever was in that thing above me. There's something bigger out there, a spiritual Being that pulls the strings on all the wee folk here and above. Maybe it will be revealed later on, somewhere down the line..."

I can add only one more thought.

I started this book with some advice for my four-year-old daughter, Ashley (nicknamed "Vern"), so I should end it the same way.

As I finish writing this book, the deep green mountains through which I had traveled all during this remarkable summer have now begun to change their colors. Sitting on a knoll behind my house this day, I watch as the hues of autumn slowly stitch the hills around me into endless folds of patchwork quilts not unlike those sewn by generations of Appalachian people. As with most of the others in this book, my roots in these mountains span time and space, and surely seem connected to some greater pulse.

I reflect back to my visit in Elk Garden a few weeks ago, and I recall sitting on some large rocks while I ate my lunch in solitude next to a glittering lake. I had spent the first half of the day taking photographs and interviewing people, and then walking quietly along the narrow lanes on Nethken Hill. The experiences of the morning had been humbling and even somewhat troublesome, as I had tried to grasp some meaning out of what people had told me about the curious lights over the cemeteries.

When I had finished my sandwich and was about to leave, I glanced down into the water and was surprised to see a number of young fingerlings scurrying about. The tiny fish would dart from under the rocks in an effort to snag a crumb which had fallen from my sandwich, but seldom were they successful. It seemed as though each time they courageously moved forward, they would enter into a pool of harsh reflections cast by the bright sunlight overhead, and would turn and flee back to safety beneath the rocks.

As I ponder their actions now, weeks afterward, I wonder if I, too, have retreated when faced with the unknown. One need not get too deeply involved with UFO research before the reflections cast by such an enigmatic phenomenon become highly distorted and charged with mystery and fear. There is no doubt that sometimes I have recoiled back into the safety of my fixed reality, quite secure in the denial of what I have seen and heard.

But, like the fish, I have learned that safety does not always satisfy a hunger.

So, today, I gaze at the sky and follow the horizon to a distant hill where a man named Loomis once sent a call to the heavens.

And on a day like this, when earth and sun and sky and life are perfect in every way, I hear the answer in the wind.

It's about free will, Vern. Live, love, say your prayers and be happy. It's the *human* way.

UFO Matrix of Belief

The following is a matrix of the spectrum of scenarios found in current literature which are used to try to explain so-called UFO or ETI activity, or the lack thereof. Each matrix entry has a supporting constituency. Some of these constituencies are quite vocal, and others less so, but each are apparently confidant that their current belief structures are the most reasonable, given the data which are generally accepted. There most certainly is a large minority which is not willing to commit to one matrix entry over another, or in combination, until additional data are available.

0.   All sightings except for a small minority which lack detail can be explained in terms of naturally occurring phenomena.

1.   Craft from off planet, but from the visible universe.

2.   Interdimensional penetrations by intelligent life-forms, based in or operating from another (parallel) overlapping dimension than our own space-time.

3.   Earth-based "others," referenced throughout history, who may be other life-forms, or predominately resident in realms or dimensions we term spiritual.

4.   Hoaxes or dramatic scenarios perpetrated by various intelligence organizations as part of broader security or disinformation campaigns.

5.   Broader social engineering, or population mind-influencing programs, designed to promote a more universal planetary consciousness and to reduce the influence of nationalistic or religious traditions.

6.   Any combination of the above, including "all of the above." Intent: unknown.

UFO MATRIX OF **B**ELIEF (CONTINUED)

Possible U.S. Government levels of awareness, involvement and/or control of the phenomena termed UFO.

0.   No activity, inasmuch as the phenomena are explained by naturally occurring events.

1.   Aware, but not directly involved or in contact with the perpetrating forces.

2.   In contact to some degree, and cooperating with at least some of the source-phenomena or entities, either for technology trading or because government believes it has no choice.

3.   Government is the perpetrator of at least some of the phenomenology, perhaps drawing on the source experience for ideas and methods, but employing the events for other purposes, such as intelligence, disinformation or to alarm other nations.

4.   At least some UFO phenomena are results of government or other agency sponsored experiments in mind-control, or social control experiments or initiatives.

Note: The Human Potential Foundation, Inc. does not endorse any of the entries of the preceding Matrix of Belief. The Matrix has been prepared to stimulate discussion and research into the broad spectrum of ideas that are represented in current literature addressing what are popularly known as UFO phenomena.

West Virginia UFOs:
Close Encounters In The Mountain State

BIBLIOGRAPHY

Allen, Thomas B. *Possessed*, New York, NY., Bantam Books, 1994.

Alnor, William M. *UFOs In The New Age*, Grand Rapids, MI., Baker Book House Company, 1992.

Andrews, George C. *Extra-Terrestrial Friends And Foes*, Lilburn, GA., IllumiNet Press, 1993.

Appleby, Thomas. *Mahlon Loomis Inventor of Radio*, Washington, DC., Loomis Publications, 1967.

Baldwin, William J., D.D.S., Ph.D. *Spirit Releasement Therapy: A Technique Manual*, Falls Church, VA., Human Potential Foundation Press, 1993.

Brooke, Tal. *When The World Will Be As One*, Eugene, OR., Harvest House Publishers, Inc. 1989.

Bramley, William. *The Gods of Eden*, New York, NY., Avon Books, 1993.

Gaddis, Vincent H. *American Indian Myths & Mysteries*, New York, NY., Indian Head Books, 1992.

Graham, Rev. Billy. *Angels, God's Secret Agents*, Dallas, TX., Word Publishing, 1986

Grof, Stanislav. *Beyond The Brain*, Albany, New York, State University of New York Press, 1985.

Holroyd, Stuart. *Alien Intelligence*, New York, NY., Everest House Publishers, 1979.

Keel, John A. *The Mothman Prophecies*, Avondale Estates, GA., IllumiNet Press, 1991.

Little, Gregory L. *People of the Web*, Memphis, TN., White Buffalo Books, 1990.

Mack, John E., M.D. *Abduction, Human Encounters With Aliens*, New York, NY., Charles Scribner's Sons, an imprint of Simon & Schuster, © 1994.

North, E. Lee. *Redcoats, Redskins, and Red-Eyed Monsters*, Cranbury, NJ., A.S. Barnes and Co., Inc. 1979.

Pacheco, Nelson S., Ph.D. and Blann, Tommy R. *Unmasking The Enemy*, Distributed by Bendan Press, Inc., Arlington, VA., 1994.

Savage, Lon. *Thunder in the Mountains*, Charleston, WV., Jalamap Publications, Inc., 1984

Spencer, John. *The UFO Encyclopedia*, New York, NY., Avon Books, 1993.

Steiger, Brad and Steiger, Sherry Hansen. *Star Born*, New York, NY., The Berkley Publishing Group, 1992.

Thompson, Keith. *Angels and Aliens, UFOs and the Mythic Imagination*, Reading, MA., Addison-Wesley Publishing Company, Inc., 1991.

Valerian, Valdamar. *Matrix*, ©1992, Port St. Lucie, FL., Arcturus Books.

Vallee, Jacques. *Passport To Magonia*, Chicago, IL., Contemporary Books, 1993.

Vallee, Jacques. *Revelations*, New York, NY., Ballantine Books, 1992.

West Virginia County Maps, Lyndon Station, WI., Thomas Publications, LTD.

The World Almanac and Book of Facts, Mahwah, NJ., World Almanac, Funk & Wagnalls, 1993.

HEADLINE BOOKS, INC.

West Virginia Proud

A New Voice In Publishing
From The World's Oldest Mountains

Use This Handy Order Form To Order Additional Copies

West Virginia UFOs:
Close Encounters In The Mountain State

Name or Company Name:_____

Street Address:_____

Suite or Apartment #:_____

City, State & Zip Code:_____

To The Attention of:_____

Quantity Desired:_____ (Quantity Discounts Available to Booksellers)

Pricing Information:

For West Virginia Residents: Each book is $18.35 (includes 90-cents sales tax and a postage / handling charge of $2.50).

For Orders Outside of West Virginia: Each book is $17.45 (includes a postage / handling charge of $2.50).

Mail your check or money order to:

Headline Books, Inc.
P. O. Box 52
Terra Alta, WV 26764